Life in a
Medieval Castle

Chepstow Castle, with the River Wye in the right background: At the eastern end of the castle (to the right), Marten's Tower and the great gatehouse, leading to the lower bailey or courtyard, flanked on the side toward the river by the thirteenth-century living quarters. Beyond, a gate guarded by a round tower leads to the middle bailey. At the narrowest point of the ridge rises the Great Tower, built about 1070. Beyond it, the upper bailey leads to the barbican (advance fortification) and western gatehouse. (Department of the Environment, U.K.)

Life in a Medieval Castle

Joseph and Frances Gies

Thomas Y. Crowell Company
NEW YORK / ESTABLISHED 1834

Excerpts from *Gesta Stephani* are quoted from K. R. Potter's translation, published by Thomas Nelson and Sons, Ltd., London, in 1955; those from Andreas Capellanus' *De Amore* are taken from J. J. Parry's translation, *The Art of Courtly Love*, published by Columbia University Press, New York, in 1941; excerpts concerning Robert of Flanders' money-fief, John of Toul's multiple homage, and Frederick Barbarossa's law forbidding the sale of fiefs are from *Feudalism*, by Joseph Strayer, copyright © 1965, reprinted by permission of D. Van Nostrand Company; the three medieval songs are reproduced from *New Oxford History of Music*, Volume II, ed. Dom Anselm Hughes, published by the Oxford University Press, London, in 1954; the verses from William IX's poem are reprinted from Hubert Creekmore's *Lyrics of the Middle Ages*, Grove Press, New York, 1959; the letters of Simon of Senlis, Eleanor de Montfort's household accounts, the story of the siege of Bedford, and the English oath of homage are taken from Margaret Hennings' *England Under Henry III*, published by Longmans, Green, London, 1924.

Illustration on page 173 and two on page 193 are from *British Castles*, by R. J. Unstead, published by the Thomas Y. Crowell Company (originally published as *Castles* by A. & C. Black, Ltd., London, 1970). Department of the Environment photographs, British Crown copyright, are reproduced by permission of the Controller of Her Britannic Majesty's Stationery Office.

Designed by Ingrid Beckman
Manufactured in the United States of America

ISBN 0-690-00561-X

Library of Congress Cataloging in Publication Data
Gies, Joseph.
    Life in a medieval castle.

    Bibliography: p. 249.
    1. Castles. 2. Courts and courtiers. 3. Chepstow Castle. I. Gies, Frances, joint author. II. Title.
GT3520.G53   914'.03'1   74-13058
ISBN 0-690-00561-X

1   2   3   4   5   6   7   8   9   10

By the Authors

To Lynn, who builds castles

Acknowledgments

The authors wish to express their thanks to Professor C. Warren Hollister of the University of California at Santa Barbara for his helpful suggestions and corrections, and to the Northwestern University Library, the British Museum, and the British Department of the Environment.

Contents

Illustrations

Prologue: Chepstow Castle

NORTH OF THE NEW SEVERN SUSPENSION BRIDGE, on the Welsh border in Monmouthshire, Chepstow Castle rises from a narrow ridge commanding the River Wye, a broad, shallow stream that fluxes daily with the tidal Severn from a navigable river to a nearly dry mud flat.

From the opposite bank of the Wye, the castle presents the image of a rugged and almost intact stone fortress, of immense length (nearly seven hundred feet), oriented east-west, its battlemented walls buttressed by several powerful towers, both square and cylindrical. The stone, varying from gray limestone to yellow and dark red sandstone, reinforces the towers' suggestion of more than one period of construction.

Entry to the castle is through the Great Gatehouse at the eastern end, leading to a large grassy courtyard some two hundred feet square. South from the gatehouse extends a forty-foot-high wall that ends at the castle's southeast corner in an enormous tower, flat on the inner side, semicircular on the outer, known as Marten's Tower, a designation it acquired late in its history when Henry Marten, a seventeenth-century political prisoner, was confined in it for the last twenty years of his life. On the north side, facing Marten's Tower, an array of thirteenth-century buildings known as the domestic range hugs the wall overlooking the river. Examined more closely, the domestic range resolves into two large stone halls, with chambers, cellars, storerooms, and—positioned directly over the river—latrines.

This easternmost court is known as the Lower Bailey. Beyond it to the west, with access through a tower-guarded inner gate, lies the Middle Bailey, another walled enclosure. At its farther end, oriented like the entire castle east and west and almost completely occupying the narrowest part of the ridge, rises the Great Tower. Now a floorless, roofless shell with half its upper story destroyed, the Great Tower is the oldest part of Chepstow, originally built in the eleventh century, and until the construction of the domestic range the center of the castle's life. Twice remodeled, with a third story added to its initial two, Chepstow Castle in its earliest form can here be identified by masonry and architectural detail: huge yellow stone blocks in the base supporting walls of smaller, rougher yellow stone, pierced by small round-headed (Romanesque) windows and doorways with similar arches, or with square lintels. The first remodeling, in the second quarter of the thirteenth century, marked by rough limestone masonry, added a third story to the western third of the tower and enlarged the openings of the second story, converting them into pointed-arch (Gothic) windows and doors, with elaborate carved decoration. The final addition late in the thirteenth century of the eastern two-thirds of the upper story is indicated by the use of roughly-squared rubble and red sandstone.

On the northern side of the Great Tower runs a

Chepstow Castle: The great (eastern) gatehouse and Marten's Tower.
(Department of the Environment)

passageway known as the Gallery, once timber-covered, squeezed between the Great Tower and the wall fronting the river. Another fortified gate (now gone) once guarded the entrance from the Gallery into the third and western-most courtyard, the Upper Bailey, at the end of which stands a rectangular tower built to command the western gateway of the castle. This entry was further strengthened by the addition of an outer walled enclosure, or barbican, with its own gatehouse, marking the western extremity of the castle.

Despite the disappearance of timber roofs, floors, and outbuildings and the dilapidation of the upper part of some walls and towers, Chepstow Castle is exceptionally well

CHEPSTOW CASTLE

KEY

A. site of screens
B. buttery
C. pantry
D. porch
E. cellar
F. buttery
G. passage
H. pantry
I. garde-robe
J. servery
K. oven
L. chamber (upper)

M. prison
N. great gatehouse
O. site of possible barbican
P. guard room
Q. Marten's Tower
R. well
S. earth filling
T. postern
U. inner walls of tower demolished
V. postern
W. upper gatehouse
X. site of gate
Y. gallery

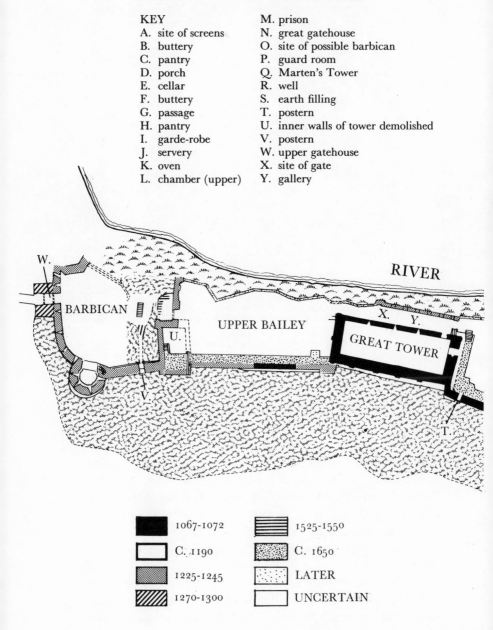

	1067-1072		1525-1550
	C. 1190		C. 1650
	1225-1245		LATER
	1270-1300		UNCERTAIN

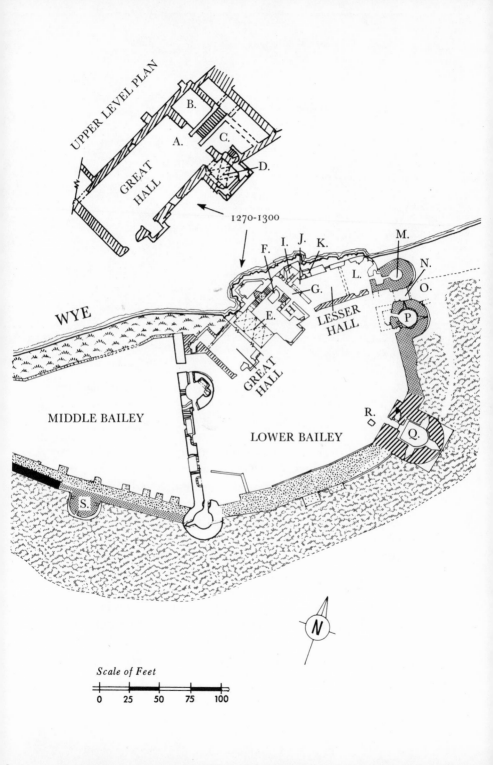

UPPER LEVEL PLAN

B.

A.

C.

GREAT HALL

D.

1270-1300

WYE

F. I. J. K.

M.

N.

O.

G.

L.

P.

E. H.

LESSER HALL

GREAT HALL

MIDDLE BAILEY

R.

Q.

LOWER BAILEY

S.

N

Scale of Feet

0   25   50   75   100

Chepstow Castle: The western gatehouse and barbican. On the right, the eleventh-century Great Tower. (Department of the Environment)

preserved. In size, strength, and setting, it is one of the most imposing of the great medieval castles of Europe, the more impressive for the fact that it is unmarred by modern restoration. Its assemblage represents three centuries of castle-building; its lords were four powerful Anglo-Norman families. The weathered stones speak in unmistakable accents of an age of hardihood, few comforts, and much danger, an age dominated by Chepstow and all the other castles from Scandinavia to Italy. Everywhere in Europe in the High Middle Ages the castle played a crucial role: military, political, social, economic, cultural. In England an extraordinary historical context made its career especially dramatic, and England today has one of the richest collections of medieval castle ruins of all the lands where castles appeared—one authority asserts there are remnants of at least fifteen hundred.

· How such castles came to be built, their function in history, and especially the life that filled them during their thirteenth-century day of glory, is the subject of this book. Because Chepstow illustrates many of the features of castle architecture and living arrangements, and because its lords were among the foremost barons of their time, the story will center around Chepstow. Other castles, in England and on the Continent, will also be freely drawn on, since the exploration of one castle, even a Chepstow, does not suffice to illustrate all the many facets of the life within and surrounding the medieval castle.

I

The Castle Comes to England

ON THE MORNING OF SEPTEMBER 28, 1066, nearly a thousand double-ended, open longboats, each mounting a single square sail, suddenly appeared off the coast of England at Pevensey, about forty miles southwest of Dover. As the boats ran up on the beach, some seven thousand armed men leaped from them and waded ashore. The army of Duke William of Normandy, after waiting weeks for a favorable wind, had crossed seventy miles of water in a single night to enforce their leader's claim to the English throne. Recruited not only from his own vassals in Normandy, but from mercenaries and adventurers throughout northern France and even farther away, it was for the eleventh century not only a very large but an exceptionally well disciplined force, a tribute to the authority as well as the financial resources of Duke William.

England had seen many seaborne invading forces, but

probably never one this large. A novel feature of Duke William's amphibious army was its horses, no fewer than three thousand of which had been successfully ferried across the Channel by means of a technique—probably some kind of sling-harness—that Norman soldiers of fortune apparently learned from the Byzantine Greeks. Carried in the flotilla was a prefabricated fort, the timbers cut, shaped, framed, and pinned together in France, dismantled, packed in great barrels, and loaded on the ships. Disembarking at Pevensey, the Normans had the reassembled fort complete by evening.

The timber fort at Pevensey was an omen. Norman chronicler Ordericus Vitalis made the highly significant observation that in Saxon England there were "but few of the fortresses which the Normans call castles." The whole of England in 1066 had perhaps half a dozen: one in Essex, near the east coast; three in Hereford, near the Welsh border; one at Arundel, in Sussex, near the Channel (all built by Norman knights in the service of Edward the Confessor); and finally, one at Dover, built by Edward's successor and William's rival, King Harold Godwinson. Most if not all of these were of timber and earthwork, like nearly all the castles on the Continent.

Jean de Colmieu described the typical "motte-and-bailey" castle of northern France:

> It is the custom of the nobles of the neighborhood to make a mound of earth as high as they can and then encircle it with a ditch as wide and deep as possible. They enclose the space on top of the mound with a palisade of very strong hewn logs firmly fixed together, strengthened at intervals by as many towers as they have means for. Within the enclosure is a house, a central citadel or keep which commands the whole circuit of the defense. The entrance to the fortress is across a bridge . . . supported on pairs of posts . . . crossing the ditch and reaching the upper level of the mound at the level of the entrance gate [to the enclosure].

Berkhamsted Castle: The contours of William the Conqueror's original motte-and-bailey castle are clearly seen, now that the later stonework is in ruins. The motte (mound) was crowned with a timber stockade. Berkhamsted was unusual in having a wet moat. (Aerofilms, Ltd.)

Requiring no skilled labor, such motte-and-bailey castles were quick and cheap to construct. They had a further advantage in that they were basically independent of considerations of terrain, and could be built anywhere that a fortification was needed. The motte, or mound, was steep-sided, sometimes partly natural, sometimes wholly artificial, formed in part by soil from the encircling ditch. Flat-topped, roughly circular, usually one hundred to three hundred feet in diameter at the base and anywhere from ten to one hundred feet high, the motte was crowned by a wall of timber palisades. The "central citadel or keep" was hardly more than a blockhouse or tower, usually of wood, though occasionally, where stone was plentiful, of masonry. The tower was too small to house more than the lord or the commander (castellan) of the castle and his immediate

family, and the entire space of the motte was too restricted
to accommodate the garrison with its animals and supplies
except on an emergency basis.

Therefore a much larger space was cleared below the
motte, given its own ditch and palisade, and connected to
the upper fort by an inclined trestle with a drawbridge.
This lower court, or bailey, was roughly circular or oval, its
exact shape depending on the contours of the land.
Sometimes there were two baileys, or even three, in front of
the mound or on either side of it. The sense of the
arrangement was that the garrison could use the whole
interior of motte and bailey for everyday living, secure
against minor attacks. In case of a serious threat, the
garrison crowded up into the steep-walled motte.

Despite their scarcity in England, such motte-and-bailey
castles were numerous on the Continent. Fortification was,
of course, an ancient art, widely practiced even in pre-
Roman Europe. The castle built by King Harold at Dover
occupied the site of (and made use of) a Roman fort that
had itself taken over the site of a much earlier Iron Age
stronghold. The Roman legions were famed for their skill at
fortification, building ditched and walled ramparts in a
matter of hours at whatever point they encamped. If a
legion remained long in one place, it habitually turned the
temporary *castrum* into a permanent stone fortress. At least
eight other Roman fortresses besides Dover dotted the old
"Saxon shore" of eastern England to fend off third- and
fourth-century pirates. Elsewhere, too, the Romans built
large stone fortresses, often taking advantage, as at Dover,
of Iron Age ruins. The immense fortified village of Old
Sarum was another such Roman renewal of older works.

Nevertheless, the Roman constructions were not really
castles in the sense of a later day. They were forts built to be
manned by large professional garrisons, and consequently
they were not required to have great intrinsic defensive
strength. Essentially they were all, like the largest Roman

fortification in England, Hadrian's Wall, of value only as long as they were fully manned.

The *burhs* built by the Romans' Saxon successors were similarly fortifications but not castles—communally owned, walled enclosures protecting towns, each encompassing a much larger area than that of a castle, and defended by a large garrison. The ancestor of the true castle, capable of defense by a small garrison, was pioneered by the "Eastern Romans," the Byzantine Greeks, especially during the sixth-century campaigns of Belisarius in North Africa. Ain Tounga, built in Tunisia, consisted of a polygonal wall of thick masonry, with high towers at the corners and a gate tower to protect the entrance. One of the corner towers was elaborated to serve as the garrison's ultimate refuge, or as the Europeans who adopted the Byzantine model a few centuries later called it, the "keep" or "donjon." The Muslims adopted the Byzantine art of masonry fortification, using it in Spain in the eighth and ninth centuries to build hundreds of hilltop castles strengthened by square towers, a form later imitated by the Christians in the Reconquest.

The true castle—the private fortress—first appeared in northwest Europe in the ninth century, by no coincidence the period of the devastating raids by Vikings and Saracens. By 863, when Charles the Bald, Charlemagne's grandson, ordered castles to be built against the invaders, castle-building was probably already under way. The decentralized character of the Carolingian state dictated that the new strongholds should be for the most part in the hands of dukes, counts, and barons who lived in them with their families, servants, and armed retainers. Technology and economics determined that they be constructed of earth and wood. Rough-and-ready motte-and-bailey castles sprang up all over France, Germany, Italy, and the Low Countries.

Castle construction had a profound effect on the European political scene. Not only could a castle block invasion of a region, but it could also provide effective control over the local population. Both aspects of the castle were well understood in Continental Europe, where the owners of castles were soon unchallenged owners of power.

Yet when William invaded England, King Harold, whose castles were few and scattered, had to put his kingdom at hazard on the result of a single pitched battle. His army fought well at Hastings through the long bloody day of October 14, but in the end it was overcome, apparently after a ruse by the Norman horsemen, who pretended to flee and drew some of the defenders down from their hillside position. King Harold was slain along with his two brothers and most of his best troops.

The intensity of the battle and its decisive character were typical of eleventh-century fighting. Two battles just fought in the north, Harold Hardraada's victory over the earls of Mercia and Northumberland at Gate Fulford, and Harold Godwinson's victory over Hardraada at Stamford Bridge, had been very similar. Evidently the relative ineffectiveness of missile weapons forced eleventh-century armies to engage at close quarters. It is not surprising, therefore, that despite his own severe losses William found himself on October 15 in command of the only serious fighting force in England.

In addition, the death of Harold and his brothers left William with a virtually uncontested claim to the throne. Yet the ease with which he now completed the conquest of England is astonishing, and was certainly due in no small measure to the scarcity of English castles. Of those that did exist, only Dover was situated to embarrass William, and Dover surrendered at his approach, probably because its garrison had fought and been destroyed at Hastings.

His coastal base secure, William turned west, and after a tentative raid on London by some of the cavalry, moved in a wide arc to cut the capital off from the interior. With no castle to obstruct his movements, he swung his army completely around London from southeast to northwest, and the isolated city submitted. On Christmas Day William was crowned, and had himself presented to his new subjects by the archbishop of York, speaking English, and the bishop of Coutances, speaking French. Londoners were promptly set to work to build a castle. Inside the Roman city walls, on the Thames shore between the city and the sea, this original Tower of London was apparently of earth and timber. It was replaced a dozen years later by the square stone bulk of the White Tower.

When early in 1067 William left England for a stay in Normandy, he took additional precautions, completing another castle, at Winchester, the most important city in southwest England, and entrusting it to William Fitz Osbern, described by Ordericus Vitalis as "the best officer in his army" and "the bravest of all the Normans." The king gave Dover Castle—much strengthened—and the Kent countryside into the hands of his own half-brother, Odo, bishop of Bayeux, and made the two men co-justiciars, or regents, with the task of extending the castle complex outward from the Dover-London-Winchester triangle. The native population was ruthlessly conscripted for labor service. Fitz Osbern and Odo "wrought castles widely throughout the land and oppressed the poor people," soberly recorded *The Anglo-Saxon Chronicle*.

During William's absence, an insurrection broke out in the southeast that gained support from Count Eustace of Boulogne, a disaffected French baron, revealing an unforeseen potential danger to the regime. The rebellion failed in its objective of capturing Dover Castle, and the castle garrison, by a surprise sortie, routed the rebels. On Christmas of 1067 William was back in England, but the next

Tower of London: The White Tower, the rectangular stone keep begun about 1077 by William the Conqueror. (Department of the Environment)

three years saw several fresh insurrections, sometimes abetted by foreign aid from Denmark, Scotland, and Wales. William's response was unvarying: to suppress the rebels and to build a new castle on the spot. "He gave the custody of castles to some of his bravest Normans," wrote Ordericus, "distributing among them vast possessions as inducements to undergo cheerfully the toils and perils of defending them."

After Hastings, William had seized the estates of Anglo-Saxon landowners killed in the battle to reward his chief lieutenants, but had left most of the lands of the English nobility untouched. Now he confiscated English lands right and left, "raising the lowliest of his Norman followers to wealth and power," as Ordericus noted. Several thousand separate English holdings were combined into fewer than two hundred great estates called honors, nearly all in the hands of Normans. Where an original English landholder retained possession, he was dropped one level in the feudal hierarchy, becoming subject to a Norman lord who held his honor as a tenant-in-chief of the king. The entire county of Hereford, on the border of Wales, fell to William Fitz Osbern, the duke's faithful right hand. Fitz Osbern transferred his headquarters from Dover to Chepstow, or Striguil, as it was sometimes called, from a Welsh word meaning "the bend" (in the River Wye).

Either because of the rocky site or the strategic location, or both, Fitz Osbern determined to build his castle of stone. The rectangular keep that rose on the narrow ridge above the Wye was consequently one of the strongest in Norman England, its menacing bulk suggesting not merely a barrier to contain the Welsh but a base for aggression against them.

Dover Castle: Rectangular keep built in the 1180s. (Department of the Environment)

Chepstow Castle: Entrance to the Great Tower, with round-headed doorway decorated with Norman sawtooth carving. Below, the Great Tower from the east. The River Wye is on the right, while the towers of the barbican can be seen beyond and to the left. (Department of the Environment)

Chepstow was one of the few Anglo-Norman castles not sited to command an important town. Sometimes instead of a city causing a castle to be built, the reverse was true, as craftsmen and merchants settled close by for protection and to serve the castle household. One English example of such a castle-originated city is Newcastle-on-Tyne, which grew up around the stronghold built by William the Conqueror's son Robert to command the Tyne crossing. Several of the chief cities of Flanders were castle-derived: Ghent, Bruges, Ypres.

By 1086, when at William's orders the elaborate survey of his conquered territory known as *The Domesday Book* was compiled, the iron grip of the invading elite was beyond shaking. Only two native Englishmen held baronies as tenants-in-chief of the king in the whole of England from Yorkshire south. English chronicler William of Malmesbury commented, "Perhaps the king's behavior can be excused if he was at times quite severe with the English, for he found scarcely any of them faithful. This fact so irritated his fierce mind that he took from the greater of them first their wealth, then their land, and finally, in some instances, their lives."

William died the following year, 1087, bequeathing to his elder son, Robert, the rich old domain of Normandy, and to his younger son, William Rufus, the family's new realm of England. But though the English were now docile under their immense bridle of castles, the castles were now showing another aspect. Unchallenged centers of local power, they corrupted the loyalty of their Norman owners, who threw off their feudal obligations to assert the rights of petty sovereigns. In 1071 loyal William Fitz Osbern had been killed fighting in Flanders and his estates divided between his sons, the younger, Roger de Breteuil, inheriting his father's English lands, including Chepstow Castle. In 1074 Roger and his brother-in-law, the Breton Ralph de Guader, earl of Norfolk, had organized a rebellion, "forti-

fying their castles, preparing arms and mustering soldiers."
King William crushed this rebellion of his Norman followers like so many previous English outbreaks, and made an
effort to conciliate its leaders. To the captive lord of
Chepstow he sent an Easter box of valuable garments, but
sulky Roger threw the royal gifts into the fire. Roger was
then locked up for life and Chepstow Castle confiscated.

By the turn of the twelfth century the half dozen English
castles of 1066 had grown to the astounding number of
more than five hundred. Most were of timber, but over the
next century nearly all were converted to masonry as a
revolution in engineering construction swept Europe. New
techniques of warfare and the increasing affluence of the
resurgent West, giving kings and nobles augmented revenues from taxes, tolls, markets, rents, and licenses, brought a
proliferation of stone fortresses from the Adriatic to the Irish
Sea.

A major contributor to the sophistication of the new
castles was the extraordinary event known to the late
eleventh century as the Crusade, and to subsequent generations as the First Crusade. Of the peasants and knights who
tramped or sailed to the Holy Land and survived the
fighting, most soon returned home. The defense of the
conquered territory was therefore left to a handful of
knights—primarily the new military brotherhoods, the
Templars and the Hospitallers. Inevitably their solution
was the same as that of William the Conqueror, but the
castles they built were from the start large, of complex
design, and of stone. The Crusaders made use of the
building skills of their sometime Greek allies and their
Turkish enemies, improved by their own experience. The
results were an astonishing leap forward to massive, intri-
cately designed fortresses of solid masonry. The new model
of castle spread at once to western Europe, including
England.

Langeais: Ruins of the rectangular keep built on the Loire by Fulk Nerra of Anjou around A.D. 1000, the earliest stone keep extant in northern Europe. (Archives Photographiques)

On the Continent, even before the Crusade, where conditions were favorable, powerful keeps were sometimes built of stone, like that constructed by Fulk Nerra at Langeais on the Loire about A.D. 1000 or Brionne Castle in Normandy (early eleventh century), or like the keeps built by the Normans after their conquest of southern Italy and Sicily in the eleventh century. The baileys that accompanied such stone keeps were probably defended by timber stockades. Between the Conquest and the Crusade a few stone castles appeared in England.

Some of the new structures were conversions of motte-and-bailey castles to "shell keeps" by the erection of a stone wall to replace the timber stockade atop the motte. Within

Loches: Rectangular keep built about 1020, on the Indre River, France.
(Archives Photographiques)

Loches, interior of rectangular keep. (Archives Photographiques)

this new stone wall, living quarters were built, usually of timber, either against the wall to face a central courtyard or as a free-standing tower or hall.

In many cases the mound was too soft to support a heavy stone wall, and the new stronghold had to be erected on the lower, firmer ground of the bailey. These new keeps were usually rectangular in plan. Sometimes they were built on high or rocky ground, but site was still not a significant factor. All over northern France in the eleventh century new rectangular stone keeps rose on low or high ground, while in England William Fitz Osbern's castle at Chepstow was joined by the White Tower of London and the keeps at Canterbury and Colchester. The old wooden palisades of the bailey were now replaced by a heavy stone "curtain wall," made up of cut stone courses enclosing a rubble core and "crenelated," that is, crowned with battlements of alternating solid parts (merlons) and spaces (crenels), creating a characteristic square-toothed pattern. The curtain wall was further strengthened with towers.

In the twelfth century rectangular stone keeps continued to multiply—in England at Dover, Kenilworth, Sherborne, Rochester, Hedingham, Norwich, Richmond, and elsewhere, with thick walls rising sixty feet or more. Usually entrance was on the second story, reached by a stairway built against the side of the keep and often contained in and protected by a forebuilding. The principal room, the great hall, was on the entrance floor, with chambers opening off it; the ground floor, windowless or with narrow window slits, was used for storage. A postern or alternate gate, protected by towers, frequently opened on another side of the curtain. A well, often descending to a great depth, was an indispensable element of a keep, its water pipe carried up through two or three floors, with drawing places at each floor.

Gradually experience revealed a disadvantage in the rectangular keep. Its corners were vulnerable to the sapper,

Gisors, Normandy: Early twelfth-century shell keep built on an artificial motte 45 feet high, with a four-story octagonal tower added by Henry II of England.

or miner, and the battering ram, and afforded shelter to attackers in the form of "dead ground" that defensive fire could not reach. The Byzantines and Saracens were the first to build circular or multiangular towers, presenting no screen to the enemy at any point. But the rectangular plan remained more convenient for organizing interior space, and the European transition was gradual. For a while engineers experimented with keeps that were circular on the outside and square on the inside. Or keeps were built closely encircled by a high wall called a chemise. Entry was by a gateway in the chemise, from which one climbed a flight of steps against its interior face, and the steps led to a wall walk, which was connected to the keep by a bridge or causeway with a draw section. The drawbridge might be pulled back on a platform in front of the gate, or it might be hinged on the inner side and raised by chains on the outer so that when closed it stood vertically against the face of the gate, forming an additional barrier. Or it might turn on a horizontal pivot, dropping the inner section into the pit while the outer rose to block the gateway. An attacking enemy had to force the gate, climb the stairs, follow the wall walk, and defile across the causeway, exposed to attack from all directions.

The Tour de César in Provins, east of Paris, built in the middle of the twelfth century on the mound of an earlier motte-and-bailey, had a keep that was square below and circular above, the two elements joined by an octagonal second floor. Four semicircular turrets rose from the corners of the base, while a battlemented chemise ran around the edge of the mound and down into the bailey. Entrance was by a vaulted stairway up the mound leading to the chemise, whence a causeway and drawbridge connected with the tower itself.

Other elaborations appeared. Vertical sliding doors, or portcullises, oak-plated and shod with iron, and operated from a chamber above with ropes or chains and pulleys, enhanced the security of gateways. Machicolations—overhanging projections built out from the battlements, with openings through which missiles and boiling liquids could be dropped—were added, at first in wood, later in stone. The curtain walls were protected by towers built close enough together to command the intervening panels. Arrow loops, or *meurtrières* ("murderesses"), narrow vertical slots, pierced the curtains at a level below the battlements. Splayed, or flared to the inside, these gave the defending archer room to move laterally and so cover a broad field of fire while presenting only the narrow exterior slit as a target. A recess on the inner side sometimes provided the defender with a seat.

By the later twelfth century, older castles were being renovated in the light of the new military technology. Henry II gave Dover a great rectangular inner keep with walls eighty-three feet high and seventeen to twenty-one feet thick, with elaborate new outworks. At Chepstow the castle's most famous owner, William Marshal, built a new curtain wall, with gateway and towers, around the eastern

Fougères, Brittany: Thirteenth-century curtain wall, showing
crenelations and machicolations; Melusine and Gobelin Towers of the
thirteenth and fourteenth century in the background. Right,
machicolations of curtain wall seen from below, showing spaces through
which missiles could be dropped.

bailey, one of the earliest defenses in England to use round
wall towers and true arrow loops. In the second quarter of
the thirteenth century William's sons added the barbican
on the west, defended by its own ditch and guarded by a
tower. On the east they built a large new outer bailey, with
a double-towered gatehouse closed by two portcullises and
defended by two lines of machicolations. A successor, Roger
Bigod III, completed the fortifications by building the
western gatehouse, finished about 1272, to protect the
barbican, and constructing the great Marten's Tower at the
southeast corner of the curtain walls, begun about 1283 and
completed in the 1290s. Increased security permitted the
building of the new range of stone domestic buildings along
the north wall, including a spacious great hall, completed in
time for a visit by Edward I in December 1285.

New castles built in the thirteenth century showed even
more clearly the impact of Crusader experience. They were
sited wherever possible on the summit of a hill, with the
inner bailey backed against the more precipitous side, and

Fougères, Brittany: arrow loop in the Melusine Tower.

the main defense was constructed to face the easier slope. Two or three lines of powerful fortifications might front the approach side, making it possible, as at Chepstow, to abandon the keep as a residence for more comfortable quarters in the secure bailey. These quarters were often built of timber, while the stone keep, now usually round, and smaller but stronger, became the last line of defense and served during a siege as the lord's or castellan's command post. Stairways and passages, sometimes concealed, facilitated the movement of defense forces. Occasionally the keep was isolated within its own moat, spanned by a drawbridge, and encircled by a chemise.

In a final period, from about 1280 to 1320, some of the most powerful castles of any age or country were built in Great Britain—mainly in Wales—by Edward I. From his cousin Count Philip of Savoy, Edward borrowed an engineering genius named James of St. George, who directed a staff of engineers from all over Europe and a work force that at times numbered up to fifteen hundred. James received an excellent salary, plus life pensions for himself and his wife.

James kept the outworks of his castles strong, but concentrated the main defense on a square castle enclosed by two concentric lines of walls with a stout tower at each corner of the inner line. The keep now disappeared, rendered superfluous by the elaborate towers and gatehouses which could hold out independently even if the enemy won the inner bailey. Multiple postern gates, protected by outworks, increased flexibility. At Conway, James followed the contour of a high rock on the shore of an estuary with a wall and eight towers, and a gateway at either end protected by a barbican. Within, a crosswall divided the castle into two baileys, the outer containing the great hall and domestic offices of the garrison, the inner the royal apartments and private offices. Access was by a steep stairway over a drawbridge and through three fortified gateways under direct fire from towers and walls on every side. Caernarvon, Harlech, Flint, Beaumaris, and Denbigh

Launceston Castle, Cornwall: Shell keep built in the twelfth century by erecting a stone encircling wall on an eleventh-century motte. The round inner tower was added in the thirteenth century. (Department of the Environment)

Caerphilly Castle, Wales: Built during Edward I's conquest of Wales, on an island in a lake, Caerphilly is protected by two concentric enclosures with two powerful gatehouses at both east and west. On the more vulnerable eastern side (foreground), still a third defense was built—a long wall that dammed the entire lake and enclosed a barbican, with its own gatehouse, connected with the castle by a drawbridge. (Department of the Environment)

likewise had defenses skillfully adapted to their sites. All were built along the coast of North Wales, the wild country where the stubborn Welsh put up their stoutest resistance. In South Wales the magnificent castle of Caerphilly was built (1267–77) by Richard de Clare, earl of Gloucester, whose family had once owned Chepstow. Caerphilly's site, as picturesque as it was defensible, was on an island in a lake, surmounted by a double line of walls equipped with four powerful gatehouses, and protected by a moat and barbican with a fifth gatehouse.

Thus the castle, born in tenth-century continental Europe as a private fortress of timber and earthwork, brought to England by the Normans, converted to stone in the shell keeps and rectangular keeps of the eleventh and twelfth centuries, refined and improved by engineering knowledge from Crusading Syria, achieved its ultimate development at the end of the thirteenth century in the eastern wilds of the island of Britain.

II

The Lord of the Castle

Saxon England, nearly devoid of castles, was also devoid of most of the social and economic apparatus that typically produced the castle. "Feudalism," the term given by a later age to the dominant form of society of the Middle Ages, had in 1066 hardly made its appearance on the island of Britain. In the homeland of the Norman invaders, on the contrary, feudalism was well developed in all its aspects. These consisted of the sworn reciprocal obligations of two men, a lord and a vassal, backed economically by their control of the principal form of wealth: land. The lord—the king or great baron—technically owned the land, which he gave to the vassal for his use in return for the vassal's performance of certain services, primarily military. The vassal did not work the land himself, but gave it over to peasants to work for him under conditions that by the High Middle Ages had become institutionalized.

William and the Normans brought feudalism to England, not only because it was the social and political form they were accustomed to, but because it suited their needs in the conquered territory. William in effect laid hold of all the land in England held by secular lords—arable, forest, and swamp; took a generous share (about a fifth) for his own royal demesne; and parceled out the rest to his lay vassal followers in return for stated quotas ("fees") of knights owed him in service. The Church, which had backed the Conquest, was left in undisturbed possession of its lands, though prelates owed knights' service the same as lay lords. William's eleven chief barons received nearly a quarter of all England. Such immense grants, running to hundreds of square miles of domain, implied "subinfeudation," again the term of a later age, in which the great vassal of the king became in turn the lord of lesser vassals. In order to produce the military quota he owed the king, the lord gave his vassals "knights' fees" (fiefs) in return for their service. By the accession of Henry I in 1100 this process was far advanced, and England had become, if anything, more feudal than Normandy.

Splendidly representative of the great Norman barons of the twelfth century were the lords of Chepstow Castle. After the disgrace and imprisonment of William Fitz Osbern's son Roger, the royal power had retained possession of Chepstow, but sometime prior to 1119 Henry I granted it, with all its vast dependencies, to Walter de Clare, a kinsman and loyal stalwart of the king. Walter, remembered for founding Tintern Abbey, one of the greatest of the great English medieval monasteries, was succeeded at Chepstow by his nephew Gilbert Fitz Gilbert de Clare, who aggressively extended the family's Welsh holdings and in 1138 was made earl of Pembroke. Gilbert, surnamed Strongbow, plotted and took arms against the royal power, but turned around and came to terms with it, marrying the king's mistress, Isabel of Leicester. Their son, Richard Fitz Gilbert, also surnamed Strongbow, became one of the most renowned of all the famous Norman soldier-adventurers of his age. In 1170 this second Strongbow conquered the greater part of Ireland, taking Waterford and Dublin and restoring to power King Dermot MacMurrough of Leinster, in return for Dermot's daughter Eve and the bequest of his kingdom. On Dermot's death Strongbow made good his conquest by defending Dublin against a two-month siege by a rival Irish king, and demonstrated his loyalty (and political sagacity) by arranging to do homage for his conquest to the new king of England, Henry II (Plantagenet).

Strongbow's only son dying in childhood, his daughter Isabel became heiress for the immense holdings of the Clare family in western England, Wales, and Ireland. The choice of Isabel's husband, the new lord of Chepstow, was of obvious moment to the royal power. Henry II exercised his feudal right as lord with his habitual prudence, and Isabel was betrothed to a landless but illustrious supporter of the Crown, Guillaume le Maréchal, or William Marshal, the most admired knight of his day, and a prime example of the upward mobility that characterized the age of the castle.

William Marshal's grandfather had been an official at the court of Henry I. His name was simply Gilbert; *maréchal* ("head groom") was the name of his post. The office was sufficiently remunerative for Gilbert to defend it against rival claimants by judicial duel, and for his son John, William's father, to go a step farther and successfully assert by judicial combat that the job was hereditary. Following his victory John assumed the aristocratic-sounding name of John Fitz Gilbert le Maréchal.

In the chronicle of the civil war between Stephen of Blois (nephew of Henry I) and Matilda of Anjou (Henry I's daughter) over the English throne, John le Maréchal, or John Marshal, won mention as "a limb of hell and the root of all evil." Two instances of his hardihood especially drew the notice of the chroniclers. Choosing Matilda's side in the war, John at one moment found himself in a desperate case: to cover Matilda's retreat from a pursuing army he barricaded himself in a church with a handful of followers. Stephen's men set fire to the church, and John, with one companion, climbed to the bell tower. Though the lead on the tower roof melted and a drop splashed on John Marshal's face, putting out an eye, he refused to surrender, and when his enemies concluded that he must be dead in the smoking ruins, made good his escape.

A few years and many escapades later John was prevailed upon to hand over his young son William to the now King Stephen as a hostage against a possible act of treachery during a truce. John then went ahead and committed the treachery, reinforcing a castle the king was besieging. King Stephen threatened to hang young William unless the castle surrendered. The threat had no effect on John, who coolly answered that he did not care if his son were hanged, since he had "the anvils and hammer with which to forge still better sons."

The lad was accordingly led out next morning toward an oak tree, but his cheerful innocence won the heart of King Stephen, a man of softer mold than John Marshal. Picking the boy up, the king rode back to camp, refusing to allow him to be hanged, or—an alternative proposal from the entourage—to be catapulted over the castle wall. The king and the boy were later found playing "knights" with plantain weeds and laughing uproariously when William knocked the head off the king's plantain. Such tenderheartedness in a monarch was almost as little admired as John Marshal's brutality, *The Anglo-Saxon Chronicle* succinctly observing of Stephen that "He was a mild man, soft and good, and did no justice."

Thanks to Stephen's lack of justice, William Marshal was permitted to grow up to become the most distinguished of all the lords of Chepstow Castle and the most renowned knight of his time. Gifted with his father's soldierly prowess but free of his rascally character, William first served King Stephen and afterward his Plantagenet successor, Henry II (son of the defeated Matilda of Anjou), from whom he received Chepstow along with Isabel de Clare, the "*pucelle* [damsel] of Estriguil, good, beautiful, courteous and wise," according to William's biographer. The gift was confirmed by Henry's successor, Richard the Lionhearted, who generously (or sensibly) overlooked a past episode when William had fought Richard during the latter's rebellion against his father. As a member of the royal council, William served Richard and Richard's brother John for many years and played a leading—perhaps the leading—role in negotiating Magna Carta. On John's death he efficiently put down the rebel barons supporting Prince Louis of France and during a reluctant but statesmanlike term as regent established the boy Henry III securely on the throne.

William was succeeded as lord of Chepstow and earl of Pembroke by each of his five sons, one after the other. William Marshal II died in 1231, and was succeeded by his brother Richard, who was murdered in Ireland in 1234, possibly at the instigation of Henry III. The third son, Gilbert, died in 1241 from an accident in a tournament at Hertford. Four years later Walter Marshal succumbed, and was outlived by the fifth brother, Anselm, by only eight days. Thus was fulfilled a curse pronounced at the time of their father's death by the bishop of Fernes in Ireland. William had seized two manors belonging to the bishop's church, and the bishop had pronounced excommunication. The sentence had no effect on William Marshal, but it troubled the young king Henry III, who promised to restore the manors if the bishop would visit William's tomb and absolve his soul. The bishop went to the Temple, where William was buried, and in the presence of the king and his court addressed the dead man, as Matthew Paris commented, "as if addressing a living [person]. 'William, if the possessions which you wrongfully deprived my church of be

Pembroke Castle, Wales: Round keep built by William Marshal about 1200. (Department of the Environment)

restored . . . I absolve you; if otherwise, I confirm the said sentence that, being enmeshed in your sins, you may remain in hell a condemned man for ever.' " The king, though annoyed by the bishop's response, asked William Marshal II to return the manors. William refused, his brothers upheld his position, the young king abandoned his attempt at reconciliation, and the bishop pronounced his curse: " 'In one generation his name shall be destroyed' [in the words of the psalm] and his sons shall be without share in that benediction of the Lord, 'Increase and multiply!' Some of them will die a lamentable death, and their inheritance will be scattered." Chepstow passed out of the family by way of William's daughter Maud, who inherited after the death of Anselm in 1245.

On Maud's death in 1248, the royal power had no hand in settling the ownership of Chepstow because Maud had been a widow with grown sons. Her husband had been a Bigod, a Norman family that had risen to prominence after the Conquest. The new lord of Chepstow was Maud's oldest son, Roger Bigod, who also had the title of earl of Norfolk, and who now acquired the unique one of "earl marshal of England," an honor won by William Marshal and now officially made hereditary. The name "marshal" thus completed a cycle from designation of a job to surname to title of nobility.

Had the king been able to choose Maud's husband, he might well have passed over the Bigods, one of the most unruly families in the kingdom. Roger Bigod proved true to the tradition of his own forebears rather than to that of loyalist William Marshal. Roger joined Simon de Montfort's rebellion that wrested control of the government from Henry III, then changed sides and fought against Montfort at the battle of Lewes in 1264. Roger was succeeded by his nephew, also named Roger, who turned once more against the royal power, which he battled for many years.

Although one of their characteristics worth noting is individuality—William Marshal contrasted with the Bigods—the lords of Chepstow share a number of traits that may be taken as those of the great English lord of the High Middle Ages, and to a considerable degree, those of European lords in general. One, relatively superficial, is their Frenchness. The Clares, Marshals, and Bigods, French in origin, continued to speak French, the language of the elite, for several generations. They were French in other ways, as were the Flemish, Spanish, and German barons of the same period, France supplying not only the language of the nobility but the style—the Crusade, the *chanson de geste*, the trouvère and troubadour poetry, the tournament, the castle, the cathedral architecture.

A more deeply ingrained trait of the lords of the castles was their love of land. Even more than their much-advertised love of fighting, their dedication to getting, keeping, and enlarging their estates dominated their lives. Estate management itself, even on a smaller scale than Chepstow, was extremely demanding. No lord, however fond of fighting, could afford to neglect his estates. Many twelfth- and thirteenth-century lords passed up perfectly good wars and even stubbornly resisted participating in them because it meant leaving their lands. Few English lords, and by the thirteenth century few Continental lords, participated in the distant Crusades; they left the Holy Land to be defended mainly by Knights Templars and mercenaries. English barons even objected strenuously to fighting in defense of their king's French territories. Roger Bigod, future lord of Chepstow, and others accompanied Henry III to France only reluctantly in 1242, seizing the earliest opportunity to protest that the king had "unadvisedly dragged them from their own homes," whither they at once returned.

Land was the basis of lordship, and living on, by, and for

the land had an undoubted influence on the lord's personality. He drew his revenues from it, and used his nonfarming lands for hunting.

Politics certainly interested the lord, but nearly always because of its relation to land economics. If the sovereign's demands grew excessive, or if self-interest dictated, the baron seldom hesitated to take up arms in rebellion, his feudal oath notwithstanding. He sat on the king's council and attended what in the thirteenth century was beginning to be called parliament, partly to help the king make decisions, but mainly to look out for his own interests.

Between politics and estate management, the lord's days were typically crowded. Far from loafing in his castle during the intervals between wars, he scarcely found time to execute his many functions. At Chepstow, where the Fitz Osberns and Clares were "marcher" earls, enjoying the power that went with guarding the frontier, and where the later Marshals and Bigods had the distinction of the title of earl marshal, they exercised major functions: police, judicial, and fiscal. Such powers, delegated to the marcher earls by the king, gave them much of the independent status enjoyed by the great Continental dukes, counts, and bishops, who paid only nominal allegiance to their sovereigns and even possessed such regalian rights as that of coinage.

Most Norman barons of England were much more tightly circumscribed by the authority of the Crown. In 1086, in the setting of Roman-walled Old Sarum, William the Conqueror accepted homage and fealty from "all the landholding men of any account," that is, not only the barely two hundred tenants-in-chief but the barons' vassals. William's successors continued to encroach on baronial prerogatives. The criminal jurisdiction that traditionally belonged to large landholders was gradually usurped by the Crown. Under Henry II the Curia Regis, the royal council, assumed the role of an appeals court, as did the king's eyre (itinerant justices), whose visits to the shires to settle property suits were regularized by the later years of Henry II.

Henry II also gave decisive impetus to the jury system, which after 1166 was regularly employed to investigate crimes and to settle important civil cases. The law dispensed was a mixture of the old codes of the Saxon kings, feudal custom brought over from Normandy, and new decrees. Judgments were severe: Thieves were hanged, traitors blinded, other offenders mutilated. Sometimes a criminal was drawn and quartered. Prisoners might be confined in a castle tower or basement to await ransom or sentencing, but rarely as punishment, prison as punishment being little known in the Middle Ages. The term "dungeon" (from donjon) as a synonym for prison dates from a later era when many castles were so employed.

Though justice was summary, it was not unenlightened. Torture was not often employed even to extract confessions from thieves, confession hardly being needed if the man was caught with the goods. The records of many court cases, both civil and criminal, reveal considerable effort to determine the truth, and not infrequently a degree of lenience. By the thirteenth century the worst of the ancient barbarian legal practices were being abandoned. In 1215 the Lateran Council condemned trial by ordeal, in which a defendant strove to prove his veracity by grasping a red-hot iron without seriously burning his hand or by sinking when thrown into water, and in 1219 the custom was outlawed in England. Judicial combat, by which the defendant or his champion fought the accuser, survived longer.

On the Continent, justice was divided into high and low, with administration of high justice, comprising crimes of violence, arson, rape, kidnapping, theft, treason, counterfeiting, and false measure, generally held by the largest feudatories—kings, dukes, counts, bishops, abbots, and other great lords. The complications of the feudal system led

Chinon, on the Vienne, France: The Château du Coudray, separated from the rest of the castle by a wide moat; in the foreground the Tour du Coudray, a round keep built by Philip Augustus in the thirteenth century. The Templars were held for trial here in 1308. (Archives Photographiques)

to many special arrangements by which a lord might retain low justice, give it up to another lord, or keep only the money fines and give up the confiscations of property. Great lords, of course, did not preside over their own courts either in England or on the Continent, but were represented by provosts and seneschals.

Robbed of much of their judicial power, and thus of important revenues from the fines and confiscations, the English barons sought to compensate by acquiring posts in the royal government. The most important was that of justiciar of the realm, created by Henry I, made permanent as a kind of prime minister by Henry II, and disappearing in the thirteenth century. Other great officers of state included the chancellor, the chamberlain, the treasurer, the marshal, and the constable, backed by lesser or assistant justiciars and a throng of subordinate officials. On the local level, William the Conqueror had found an ideal policing instrument in the old Anglo-Saxon post of sheriff, chief officer of the shire (county), and had entrusted it throughout the country to his Normans.

William began by choosing his officials from among his greatest barons, such as Chepstow's William Fitz Osbern. But the tendency of many of these men, made doubly powerful by possessions and official posts, to assume independent power, induced a change of policy. Young Henry III had as his chief justiciar Hubert de Burgh, a member of a knightly family of moderate means, who acquired nearly dictatorial powers and immense wealth that apparently led to his downfall in 1232. The office of justiciar was then left vacant, and its powers passed to the chancellor.

The sheriffdom, or shrievalty, was even more a focus of conflict as the fractious barons strove to occupy it themselves or place it in friendly local hands. By the thirteenth century the office had become one of the most embattled prizes of the baronial-royal conflict. Loyal William Marshal served the king ably and faithfully as sheriff (as well as marshal, assistant justiciar, and regent), but he was an exception. More typical was ambitious, rebellious Falkes de Bréauté, who at one time held the sheriffdom in several different counties but was ultimately stripped of all office. After the baronial victory at Lewes in 1264, the barons replaced royal sheriffs wholesale, but following the royal victory at Evesham the next year, the barons' men were all turned out again. Thus the sheriff's office, which embraced important police, fiscal, and judicial functions on the county level, kept the English barons occupied in one way or another, either exercising the office or battling to control it.

On the Continent in the eighth century, the time of Charlemagne, the local government was administered in a unit much like the English one: the *pagus* or *comitatus*, counterpart of the English shire, and like the shire divided into hundreds (*centenae*), with local judicial and police powers. The court of the *pagus* was presided over either by the emperor's official, the count, or by his deputy, the viscount, the French equivalent of the sheriff. But development on the Continent followed a very different course. By the twelfth century, the *pagi* and their courts had almost disappeared, their territory and jurisdiction taken over by local feudal lords, often descendants of the old local officials, whose offices had become hereditary. In the courts of these lords most of the judicial business of the land was conducted, and they exercised most of the police and military power. In the thirteenth century the French monarchy was steadily encroaching on the great feudatories by increasing the royal domain at their expense, but the process was far from complete. Lesser barons and knights found employment in both the royal and the feudal administrations, as viscounts, bailiffs, seneschals, provosts of a town, keepers of trade fairs, and many other offices.

The great lord, even with no official post, had more than

enough to occupy him in overseeing his estates and manors and making sure his household staff did not rob him.

Underlying the social, economic, and political position of the great lord, English or Continental, were always the two pillars of feudalism: vassalage and the fief. By the thirteenth century both were hallowed, even decadent institutions, their roots in a past so far distant that few lords could give an account of them.

Vassalage was the relationship to the lord, who for all the great English barons was the king. The fief was the land granted by the lord in return for the vassal's service, or more technically, a complex of rights over the land which theoretically remained the legal possession of the lord.

The feudal relationship, which by the thirteenth century had accumulated a large train of embellishments, had originated as a simple economic arrangement designed to meet a military problem in an age when money was scarce. In late Roman times a custom had grown up whereby a man attached himself to a superior by an act of "commendation," a promise of military service in return for support, often in the form of a grant of land known as a benefice. The Frankish Carolingian rulers of the eighth century rapidly expanded this custom to meet their need for heavily armed, mounted warriors, a need that arose from the new technique of war—mounted shock combat. The enhanced military value of the mounted warrior brought a corresponding rise in his social status, symbolized by a more personal relationship between lord and vassal. This more personal relationship was in turn symbolized by a new commendation ritual reinforced by an oath of fealty. In the commendation, the vassal placed his hands within the hands of the lord. The oath was sworn on a relic—a saint's bone, hair, or scrap of garment—or on a copy of a Gospel. The contract entered into could not be lightly broken.

Charlemagne laid down precise and exceptional cases in

which the vassal might justifiably foreswear his oath: if the
lord tried to kill or wound him, to rape or seduce his wife or
daughter, to rob him of part of his land, or to make him a
serf, or, finally, if he failed to defend him when he should.
The lord had no absolute power over his vassal; if he
accused the vassal of wrongdoing, he had to accord him
trial in the public court, with the "jury of his peers."

In Charlemagne's time a vassal who owed military
service, on horseback, with full equipment, needed a
benefice amounting to from three hundred to six hundred
acres, requiring about a hundred villeins to plow, plant,
and harvest it. Although the land continued to belong
formally to the lord, custom more and more favored the
permanent retention of the land by the vassal's family. The
new vassal performed the commendation and oath as had
his father. William Longsword, ancestor of William the
Conqueror, on succeeding his father as duke of Normandy
in 927, "committed himself into the king's hands," according to the chronicler Richer, and "promised him fealty and
confirmed it with an oath." An example of the renewal of
vassalage following the death of the lord, as practiced in the
twelfth century, is recorded by Galbert of Bruges at the time
of the succession of William Clito as count of Flanders in
1127, when a number of knights and barons did homage to
the new count:

"The count demanded of the future vassal if he wished
without reserve to become his man, and he replied, 'I so
wish'; then, with his hands clasped and enclosed between
those of the count, their alliance was sealed by a kiss." The
vassal then said: "I promise by my faith that from this time
forward I will be faithful to Count William and will
maintain toward him my homage entirely against every
man, in good faith and without any deception." Galbert
concluded: "All this was sworn on the relics of saints.
Finally, with a little stick which he held in his hand, the
count gave investiture."

Homage: The vassal puts his hands between those of his lord. (Bibliothèque Nationale. MS. Fr. 5899, f. 83v)

In England the oath of homage always contained a reservation of allegiance toward the king. A thirteenth-century English legal manual cites this formula:

> With joined hands [the vassal] shall offer himself, and with his hands under his lord's mantle he shall say thus—I become thy man of such a tenement to be holden of thee, to bear to thee faith of life and member and earthly worship against all men who live and can die, saving the faith of my lord Henry king of England and his heirs, and of my other lords—if other lords he hath. And he shall kiss his lord.

The ceremonial kiss was widely used, though it was less significant than the ritual of homage and the oath of fealty.

The vassal's obligations fell into two large classes, passive and active. His passive obligations were to refrain from doing the lord any injury, such as giving up one of his castles to an enemy, or damaging his land or other property. The active duties consisted of "aid and counsel." Under the "aid" heading came not only the prescribed military duty, *ost* or host, commonly forty days with complete equipment, either alone or with a certain number of knights, but a less onerous duty, *chevauchée* or cavalcade, which might mean a minor expedition, or simply escort duty, for example when the lord moved from one castle to another. In addition there was often the important duty of castle guard, and the further duty of the vassal to hold his own castle open to the lord's visit. Highly specialized services also appeared, ranging from the obligation of the chief vassals of the bishop of Paris to carry on their shoulders the newly consecrated bishop on his formal entry into Notre Dame, to that of a minor English landholder of Kent of "holding the king's head in the boat" when he crossed the choppy Channel.

In the twelfth century a wholly new kind of service had developed that gave the vassal-lord relationship a fresh significance. This was scutage (from the Latin *scutum*, "shield"), a money payment that took the place of military service. Its appearance showed how far Europe had come since Charlemagne's time in economic sophistication. The new custom was especially conspicuous in England, where William the Conqueror had laid direct hold of the land, something quite impossible for the king of France or the emperor of Germany, whose domains were entangled in a mass of ancient feudal relationships. Richard the Lion-hearted, calling on his barons for a war in France, proposed that they each send just seven knights and fulfill the remainder of their obligations with money. The barons, averse to leaving their castles, preferred the arrangement. So did Richard. In place of self-willed vassals whose terms of service might run out the day before a battle, he got mercenary soldiers who did as they were told and stayed as long as they were paid.

Included in the "aid" part of vassalage were financial obligations entirely apart from the money substituted for military service. "Relief" was a payment made by a new tenant at the beginning of his tenancy. A new knight paid his lord one hundred shillings for his knight's fee (fief). The great lord paid a relief to the king proportionate to his holdings, sometimes running to a thousand pounds or more.

The term "aid" itself came to be used to designate certain money obligations exacted by all great lords on special occasions, three of which were widely recognized: ransom of the lord's person, marriage of his eldest daughter, and knighting of his eldest son. These three were specified in Magna Carta as all that the king of England could require of his barons. Sixty years later the Statute of Westminster (1275) fixed rates: twenty shillings of aid per each twenty pounds' worth of land held at a rent, that is, a levy of five per cent, usually twice in the lord's lifetime. A fourth aid, for going on Crusade, was widely accepted on the Continent. Aids were not restricted to baronial vassals, but were charged to many others, including the wealthy burghers of the towns, often a surer source of revenue than even the large barons.

The "counsel" part of the vassal's obligation required him to come to his lord's (i.e., in the case of a tenant-in-chief, the king's) castle when summoned, and the word counsel, or council, was soon attached to the gathering itself. A lord was expected to consult his vassals on major questions of policy, such as negotiating an important marriage or going to war. But often the purpose was to try judicial cases. Occasionally the sovereign might prefer to have someone else take the blame for offending one party or another in a dispute, and so welcomed his vassals' help, but more often the contrary was the case—that is, the sovereign's interest was served by trying his barons himself, finding them guilty, and extracting fines or expropriations. King John's abuse of this power was a prime cause of the baronial revolt that led to Magna Carta, with the specification of the already time-honored "jury of his peers" for the accused baron.

An important reciprocal obligation of every lord toward his vassals, whether the king toward his barons or a baron toward his knights, was that of defending them when they were accused in other courts—for example, in those of the Church. Self-interest dictated honoring the obligation, since any danger to a vassal's fief arising from such litigation threatened financial harm to the lord.

Vassalage was thus a many-faceted arrangement. Its

economic basis, the second component of the feudal relationship, was the fief. In the eleventh century the term, from
the Latin *feodum,* had gradually supplanted the older
"benefice" to designate the property a lord conferred on a
vassal for his maintenance. A fief might be anything that
brought in revenue—a mill, a rented house, a market with
its fees, a toll bridge, or even a saleable chattel (movable
property). Abbeys and churches often belonged as fiefs to
lay vassals who pocketed the tithes and endowments and
even sometimes the offerings of the faithful. Land, however,
was by far the commonest form of fief. In the twelfth and
thirteenth centuries western Europe, including Britain, was
covered with fiefs of sizes ranging from thousands of acres
and embracing farm, pasture, woodland, and village, down
to fiefs of a mere half dozen acres.

By the thirteenth century the feudal relationship had
become so complex through inheritances and grants that a
baron might hold his castle as a fief from one lord and much
of his land from another, and several other revenue-producing fiefs from still others. In England, because of the
Conqueror's seizure of all land, a tidy pyramid of fiefs
originally existed, with the king the sole landowner and the
great lords—the tenants-in-chief, of Chepstow and other
vast estates—the only direct fief-holders. The tenants-in-
chief sub-granted some of their lands to lesser lords and
knights, who in turn often further subdivided them. The
lords seized the opportunity to exact relief from inheriting
vassals, and by the end of the twelfth century this payment
had been widely fixed at a year's revenue of the fief. Magna
Carta set a barony's relief at one hundred pounds, and that
of a knight's fee (fief) at a maximum of five pounds.

In case of a minor succeeding to a fief, the lord in
England (and Normandy) enjoyed the revenues of the fief
until the heir was of age, with only the obligation of
protecting him. Elsewhere an older relative was commonly
assigned as protector.

"Alienation," or sale, of a fief ran counter to the whole sense of the feudal system, with its hereditary relationships, its emphasis on military-style loyalty, and its religious sanctions. Yet inevitably a commerce in fiefs developed. Inheritance might lead to holdings that could be consolidated by judicious trading. Or a poor knight might simply be desperate for money. By the twelfth century, transactions in fiefs were a recognized part of the system, with the lord merely taking care to be formally included in the document to protect his own rights against erosion. In 1159 Thierry of Alsace, the count of Flanders, issued a charter respecting the trade of a piece of land by one of his vassals for a larger tract, presumably of equal value, belonging to the church of St. Nicholas of Furnes:

> It is my wish that the following facts be known, that 45½ measures of land held of me in fief by Leonius and of the latter by his brother Guy were resigned by Guy to Leonius and by the latter to me, and that I have now given them to the church of St. Nicholas of Furnes to possess freely and for ever. And in exchange for them I have received from the church 91 measures of land which I have given to the said Leonius to be held in fief of me, and he has handed them over to his brother to hold them in fief of him.

Concern over the growing transformation of the feudal relationship was expressed by Holy Roman Emperor Frederick Barbarossa in 1158:

> We have heard bitter complaints from the princes of Italy . . . that the fiefs which their vassals hold from them are either used as security for loans or sold without the permission of their lords . . . whereby they lose the service owed, and the honor of the Empire and the strength of our army is diminished.
>
> Having taken the advice of bishops, dukes, margraves, counts . . . and other leading men, we decree, God willing, this permanent law: No one may sell or pledge the whole or

part of a fief or alienate it in any way without the consent of his lord from whom he is known to hold the fief. . . .

We also forbid those clever tricks by which fiefs are sold and money is received . . . under color of a pretended enfeoffment [granting of a fief]. . . . In such illegal contracts, both seller and buyer shall lose the fief, which then will revert to the lord. The notary who knowingly draws up such a contract shall lose his office . . . and have his hand cut off.

But the trend was too deeply embedded in the resurgent European economy to be checked. By the thirteenth century, with commerce flourishing, money abundant, and a new-rich class constantly growing, fiefs were bought and sold, except in form, like any other property. A baron whose family had held land for hundreds of years might, coming on hard times, sell some or all to a city burgher who, having made a fortune in banking or the cloth trade, wished to invest in land to protect his capital and gain entry to the aristocracy.

Another problem developing for the feudal system in the later Middle Ages was that of multiple fiefs, automatically demanding multiple homage and so destroying the ideological foundation of the system, the sworn loyalty of a subordinate to a chief. When Henry I, son of William the Conqueror, succeeded in purchasing the vassalage of Count Robert of Flanders, Count Robert spelled out the disingenuous means by which he would fulfill the agreement at the expense of his true feudal lord, the king of France:

If King Philip plans to attack King Henry in England, Count Robert, if he can, will persuade King Philip to stay at home . . . . And if King Philip invades England and brings Count Robert with him, the count shall bring as few men with him as he can without forfeiting his fief to the king of France.

. . . After Count Robert is summoned by the king of England, he shall get a thousand knights together as quickly as possible in his ports, ready to cross to England. And the

king shall find . . . enough ships for these knights, each
knight having three horses.

. . . And if King Henry wishes Count Robert to help him
in Normandy or in Maine . . . the Count shall go there with
a thousand knights and shall aid King Henry faithfully, as
his ally and lord from whom he holds a fief.

. . . And if at this time, King Philip shall attack King
Henry in Normandy, Count Robert shall go with King
Philip with only twenty knights, and all his other knights
shall remain with King Henry.

The king promises to protect Count Robert in life and
limb . . . and give as a fief to Count Robert 500 pounds of
English money every year.

In other words, Count Robert was to receive a "money
fief" of 500 pounds a year to fight on King Henry's side with
1,000 knights, or, if he was simultaneously summoned by
King Philip, to fight on both sides at once, taking the field
in person for Philip, but with only 20 knights, while sending
980 knights to fight for Henry.

The Count of Flanders was deliberately placing himself
in an awkward position in order to profit from a handsome
money payment, but many lords found themselves in
similar situations merely through their inheritances. In the
thirteenth century John of Toul had four lords, and foresaw
a variety of complications of loyalty that he tried to meet:

If it should happen that the Count of Grandpré should be
at war with the Countess and Count of Champagne for his
own personal grievances, I will personally go to the assistance
of the Count of Grandpré and will send to the Countess and
Count of Champagne, if they summon me, the knights I owe
for the fief which I hold of them. But if the Count of
Grandpré shall make war on the Countess and Count of
Champagne on behalf of his friends and not for his own
personal grievances, I shall serve in person with the Countess
and Count of Champagne and I will send one knight to the
Count of Grandpré . . . .

The significance of such dilemmas as those of Count Robert and John of Toul was not the problems created for the vassals by multiple loyalty but the freedom of choice conferred. A baron with multiple loyalties could always find a solution that met with his own self-interest. Basically, the baron enjoying a fief consisting of a strong castle and broad manors had a powerful position for bargaining with anyone. With his revenues from fines, tolls, taxes, and fees, he could maintain a high degree of independence, regardless of how lawyers described his situation.

The most powerful barons, holders of castles and fiefs from a number of lords, were the strong men of the thirteenth century, able to resist kings and emperors. Even the powerful king of England had to acknowledge their rights in Magna Carta.

William Marshal was universally praised by contemporaries for his "loyalty," that is, his unwavering fidelity to the obligations between vassal and lord, even when it came into conflict with his relations with the king. William stuck to his lord, young Henry, eldest son of Henry II, when the young man rebelled against his father; he refused to do homage to Richard the Lionhearted for the Irish lands that he held of Richard's brother John; and in 1205 he declined to fight for John against Philip Augustus, to whom he had done homage for his Norman lands. Marshal's old-fashioned feudal code, however, was beginning to come into conflict with the new stirrings of nationalism. In 1217, when as regent for Henry III he concluded a lenient peace with the invading forces of Prince Louis of France and the rebel English barons, he had to resist strong pressures from those who wanted to fight on in hopes of recovering Normandy for the English crown. While William would doubtless have been happy to recover Normandy for his sovereign, he regarded the question as academic as far as his own baronial interests were concerned, because he saw no reason why a man should not hold lands simultaneously of the king of England and the king of France. Despite his famous loyalty, "sovereignty" was to him a feebler, less material concept than "lordship." A new day was dawning, however, and emphasis shifting. After William's death, Henry criticized his moderation, and much later, in 1241, even went so far as to condemn it to one of William's sons as treachery.

In the long-drawn-out struggle of the English barons with the king, economic disputes played a major role. The barons succeeded rather better in this area than in others, while profiting from the slow but fairly steady rise in their own manorial incomes through the twelfth and thirteenth centuries. Although agricultural technology and acreage yields virtually stood still through the High Middle Ages, most lords were able to increase their revenues by improving their landholdings in various ways, usually at the expense of their peasants. The growth of towns also helped many lords to find a market for crop surpluses and even to practice regular cash-crop farming. Yet even in the High Middle Ages, the market was too weak to provide an adequate incentive for dramatic agricultural improvement, which had to await a later age.

In fact, the real enemy of the castle barons and their privileges was not the royal power but the slow, irresistible surge of economic change. The cloth merchants and other businessmen who exploited their workers, not perhaps more brutally, but more effectively than the barons did their villeins, were moving ahead in the economic race, while the lords of the countryside, in their arrogant but economically torpid castles, were standing still.

Some were not even able to do that. What happened to a baron who neglected his estates in favor of politics was demonstrated by the fate of the younger Roger Bigod, who inherited Chepstow from his uncle in 1270. An unreconstructed rebel after the baronial defeat at Evesham in 1265, Roger spent his whole substance, English, Welsh, and Irish, tilting at the monarchic power, to such effect that in the end he had to make an ignominious fiscal surrender. In return for the liquidation of his mountain of debts, improvident Roger signed over all his estates to the king, receiving them back for life only. By this arrangement Chepstow Castle passed into the royal demesne with Roger Bigod's death in 1302.

Thus came to an end for the mighty fortress on the Wye more than two centuries of history as a baronial castle, during which it sheltered through the long noontime of the feudal age some of the most powerful of the aristocracy of Norman England.

III

The Castle as
a House

WHILE MILITARY ENGINEERING WAS ELABORATING the castle's system of earthworks, palisades, walls, towers, gatehouses, barbicans, and battlements, the castle's domestic aspect was undergoing a parallel advance in the direction of comfort and privacy.

Few descriptions survive of the old motte-and-bailey castle, and only one gives information about living arrangements. Chronicler Lambert of Ardres described a timber castle hall built on a motte at Ardres, in Flanders, early in the twelfth century:

> The first story was on the ground level, where there were cellars and granaries and great boxes, barrels, casks, and other household utensils. In the story above were the dwelling and common rooms of the residents, including the larders, pantry and buttery and the great chamber in which

the lord and lady slept. Adjoining this was . . . the
dormitory of the ladies in waiting and children . . . .

In the upper story of the house were attic rooms in which
on the one side the sons of the lord of the house, when they so
desired, and on the other side the daughters, because they
were obliged, were accustomed to sleep. In this story also the
watchmen and the servants appointed to keep the house slept
at various times. High up on the east side of the house, in a
convenient place, was the chapel, decorated like the taber-
nacle of Solomon. . . . There were stairs and passages from
story to story, from the house into the [separate] kitchen,
from room to room, and from the house into the gallery,
where they used to entertain themselves with conversation,
and again from the gallery into the chapel.

So elaborate an architecture was exceptional in the
motte-and-bailey castle, which rarely had room for accom-
modations on such a scale. The usual arrangement must
have been for the lord's family to eat and sleep in a building
on top of the motte, while the kitchen, servants' quarters,
barracks, smithy, stables, barns, and storehouses occupied
the bailey. Alternatively the lord's family may have lived in
a hall in the bailey, with the motte serving solely as
watchtower and refuge.

Whether on the motte, in the bailey, inside the walls of
the shell keep, or as a separate building within the great
curtain walls of the thirteenth century, the living quarters of
a castle invariably had one basic element: the hall. A large
one-room structure with a lofty ceiling, the hall was
sometimes on the ground floor, but often, as in Fitz Osbern's
Great Tower at Chepstow, it was raised to the second story
for greater security. Early halls were aisled like a church,
with rows of wooden posts or stone pillars supporting the
timber roof. Medieval carpenters soon developed a method
of truss (triangular support) roof construction that made it
possible to eliminate the aisles, leaving a broad open space.
Windows were equipped with wooden shutters secured by

Pembroke, Wales: Hall built by William Marshal, c. 1190, with principal room on the second floor.

an iron bar, but in the eleventh and twelfth centuries were rarely glazed. By the thirteenth century a king or great baron might have "white [greenish] glass" in some of his windows, and by the fourteenth glazed windows were common.

In a ground-floor hall the floor was beaten earth, stone, or plaster; when the hall was elevated to the upper story the floor was nearly always timber, supported either by a row of wooden pillars in the basement below, as in Chepstow's Great Tower, or by stone vaulting. Carpets, although used on walls, tables, and benches, were not employed as floor coverings in England and northwest Europe until the fourteenth century. Chronicler Matthew Paris reported the reaction of Londoners in 1255 when Eleanor of Castile, wife of the future Edward I, was housed in an apartment "hung with palls of silk and tapestry, like a temple, and even the floor was covered with tapestry. This was done by the Spaniards, it being in accordance with the custom of their country; but this excessive pride excited the laughter and derision of the people." Floors were strewn with rushes and in the later Middle Ages sometimes with herbs, including basil, balm, camomile, costmary, cowslip, daisies, sweet fennel, germander, hyssop, lavender, majoram, pennyroyal, roses, mints, tansy, violets, and winter savory. The rushes were replaced at intervals and the floor swept, but Erasmus, noting a condition that must have been true in earlier times, observed that often under them lay "an ancient collection of beer, grease, fragments, bones, spittle, excrement of dogs and cats and everything that is nasty."

Entrance to the hall was usually in a side wall near the lower end. When the hall was on an upper story, this entrance was commonly reached by an outside staircase next to the wall of the keep. In some castles, as at Dover and Rochester, this staircase was enclosed in and protected by a building which guarded the entry to the keep—a "fore-building"; in others it was merely roofed over. In Fitz Osbern's keep the entrance stairway was constructed in the

Chepstow Castle: Interior of the Great Tower, built about 1070. The principal floor, marked by square holes where the floor beams were secured, was at second-story level, with a storage basement below. The third floor was added in the thirteenth century, in two successive remodelings. The fragment of arcade in the middle of the righthand wall marks the site of the original wooden partition dividing the story into hall (foreground) and chamber (background). A stairway to the battlements is concealed in and supported by a half-arch in the third story, above. (Department of the Environment)

thickness of the wall, leading from a doorway on the ground floor to the upper hall.

The castle family sat on a raised dais of wood or stone at the upper end of the hall, opposite to the entrance, away from drafts and intrusion. The lord (and perhaps the lady) occupied a massive chair, sometimes with a canopy by way of emphasizing status. Everyone else sat on benches. Most dining tables were set on temporary trestles that were dismantled between meals; a permanent, or "dormant," table was another sign of prestige, limited to the greatest lords. But all tables were covered with white cloths, clean and ample.

Lighting was by rushlights or candles, of wax or tallow (melted animal fat), impaled on vertical spikes on an iron candlestick with a tripod base, or held in a loop, or supported on wall brackets or iron candelabra. Oil lamps in bowl form on a stand, or suspended in a ring, provided better illumination, and flares sometimes hung from iron rings in the walls.

If the later Middle Ages had made only slight improvements in lighting over earlier centuries, a major technical advance had come in heating: the fireplace, an invention of deceptive simplicity. The fireplace provided heat both directly and by radiation from the stones at the back, from the hearth, and finally, from the opposite wall, which was given extra thickness to absorb the heat and warm the room after the fire had burned low. The ancestor of the fireplace was the central open hearth, used in ground-level halls in Saxon times and often on into later centuries. Such a hearth may have heated one of the two halls of Chepstow's thirteenth-century domestic range, where there are no traces of a fireplace. If so, it was probably situated below the high table and the dais, but away from the traffic of servants at the lower end of the hall. Square, circular, or octagonal, the central hearth was bordered by stone or tile and sometimes had a backing (reredos) of tile, brick, or

Rochester Castle: Arched fireplace in the wall of the third floor of the rectangular keep, built 1130. (Department of the Environment)

stone. Smoke rose through a louver, a lantern-like structure in the roof with side openings that were covered with sloping boards to exclude rain and snow, and that could be closed by pulling strings, like venetian blinds. In the fourteenth century, louvers were built to revolve according to the direction of the wind. There were also roof ventilators of pottery representing knights, kings, or priests, with smoke coming out of their eyes and mouths and the tops of their heads. A *couvre-feu* ("fire cover") made of tile or china was placed over the hearth at night to reduce the fire hazard.

When the hall was raised to the second story, a fireplace in one wall took the place of the central hearth, dangerous on an upper level, especially with a timber floor. The hearth was moved to a location against a wall with a funnel or hood to collect and control the smoke, and finally, funnel and all, was incorporated into the wall. This early type of fireplace was arched, and set into the wall at a point where it was thickened by an external buttress, with the smoke venting through the buttress. Toward the end of the twelfth century, the fireplace began to be protected by a projecting hood of stone or plaster which controlled the smoke more effectively and allowed for a shallower recess. Flues ascended vertically through the walls to a chimney, cylindrical with an open top, or with side vents and a conical cap.

At Chepstow, where the two halls of the thirteenth-century domestic range were built at ground level, the slope of the land was utilized to place the service rooms of the larger Great Hall above those of the Lesser Hall. The lower part of the Great Hall, containing the entranceway, was partitioned off to form a "screens passage." Such screens consisted at first of low wooden partitions projecting from side walls, with a curtain or movable screen covering the central opening. Later the central barrier became a permanent partition, with openings on either side. Above the screens commonly rose a musicians' gallery overlooking the hall.

On the lower side of the screens passage of the Great Hall at Chepstow, three doorways opened side by side. Two led to the two rooms with a passageway between them that comprised the service area. A buttery, for serving beverages, stood on one side; a pantry, for bread, on the other. In early days of castle building, these service rooms had been rough

Manorbier Castle, Wales: cylindrical chimneys.

huts or lean-tos, but by the twelfth century they were usually, as here, integral parts of the hall. They were equipped with shelves and benches on which food brought from the kitchen could be arranged for serving. The buttery of Chepstow's Great Hall contained a drain opening over the river, where a sink was doubtless situated. The third of the three doors opened between the buttery and pantry on a flight of stairs leading to the passage between the two halls. In one direction this passage led to a double latrine, cupboards, and steps down to a vaulted storage basement under the Great Hall, with an opening through which supplies could be drawn up from boats on the river below. In the other direction it led to the kitchen, located in a separate building in the Lower Bailey.

In the thirteenth century the castle kitchen was still

Chepstow Castle: Cupboards built into the wall of the passageway between the Great Hall and the Lesser Hall of the thirteenth-century domestic range.

generally of timber, with a central hearth or several fireplaces where meat could be spitted or stewed in a cauldron. Utensils were washed in a scullery outside. Poultry and animals for slaughter were trussed and tethered nearby. Temporary extra kitchens were set up for feasts, as for the coronation of Edward I in 1273 when a contemporary described the "innumerable kitchens . . . built" at Westminster Palace, "and numberless leaden cauldrons placed outside them, for the cooking of meats." The kitchen did not normally become part of the domestic hall until the fifteenth century.

In the bailey near the kitchen the castle garden was usually planted, with fruit trees and vines at one end, and plots for herbs, and flowers—roses, lilies, heliotropes, violets, poppies, daffodils, iris, gladioli. There might also be a fishpond, stocked with trout and pike.

Both the interior and exterior stonework of medieval castles were often whitewashed. Interiors were also plastered, paneled, or ornamented with paintings or hangings. Usually these interior decorations, like most of the comforts of the castle, began with the dais area of the hall, often the only part to be wainscoted and painted. A favorite embellishment was to paint a whitewashed or plastered wall with lines, usually red, to represent large masonry blocks, each block decorated with a flower. The queen's chamber at the Tower of London in 1240 was wainscoted, whitewashed, given such sham "pointing" or "masoning," and painted with roses. Wainscoting was of the simplest kind, vertical paneling painted white or in colors. In England the wood was commonly fir imported from Norway. In the halls of Henry III's castles, the color scheme was frequently green and gold, or green spangled with gold and silver, and many of the chambers were decorated with murals: the hall at Winchester with a map of the world, a lower chamber at Clarendon with a border of heads of kings and queens, an upper chamber with paintings of St. Margaret and the Four Evangelists and, as described in the king's building instructions, "heads of men and women in good and exquisite colors." Wall hangings of painted wool or linen that were the forerunners of the fourteenth-century tapestries were not merely adornments, but served the important purpose of checking drafts.

In the earliest castles the family slept at the extreme upper end of the hall, beyond the dais, from which the sleeping quarters were typically separated only by a curtain or screen. Fitz Osbern's hall at Chepstow, however, substituted for this temporary division a permanent wooden partition. In the thirteenth century William Marshal's sons removed the partition, making the old chamber part of the hall. They constructed a masonry arcade to support a new chamber above, with access by a wooden stair. In the last decade of the thirteenth century the new third-story chamber was extended over the entire hall.

The Great Hall of the domestic range at Chepstow had

its own chamber on the floor above, while the Lesser Hall was equipped with a block of chambers at the upper end, on three levels. Sometimes castles with ground-floor halls had their great chamber, where the lord and lady slept, in a separate wing at the dais end of the hall, over a storeroom, matched at the other end, over the buttery and pantry, by a chamber for the eldest son and his family, for guests, or for the castle steward. These second-floor chambers were sometimes equipped with "squints," peepholes concealed in wall decorations by which the owner or steward could keep an eye on what went on below.

The lord and lady's chamber, when situated on an upper floor, was called the solar. By association, any private chamber, whatever its location, came to be called a solar. Its principal item of furniture was a great bed with a heavy wooden frame and springs made of interlaced ropes or strips of leather, overlaid with a feather mattress, sheets, quilts, fur coverlets, and pillows. Such beds could be dismantled and taken along on the frequent trips a great lord made to his other castles and manors. The bed was curtained, with linen hangings that pulled back in the daytime and closed at night to give privacy as well as protection from drafts. Personal servants might sleep in the lord's chamber on a pallet or trundle bed, or on a bench. Chests for garments, a few "perches" or wooden pegs for clothes, and a stool or two made up the remainder of the furnishings.

The greatest lords and ladies might occupy separate bedrooms, the lady in company with her attendants. One night in 1238, Henry III of England had a narrow escape, reported by Matthew Paris, when an assassin climbed into his bedchamber by the window, knife in hand, but found him not there. "The king was, by God's providence, then sleeping with the queen." One of the queen's maids, who was awake and "singing psalms by the light of a candle," saw the man and alerted the household.

Sometimes a small anteroom called the wardrobe ad-

Curtained beds. (Trustees of the British Museum. MS. Claud. B.iv, f. 27v)

joined the chamber—a storeroom where cloth, jewels, spices, and plate were stored in chests, and where dressmaking was done.

In the thirteenth century, affluence and an increasing desire for privacy led to the building of small projecting "oriel" rooms to serve as a secluded corner for the lord and his family, off the upper end of the hall and accessible from the great chamber. Often of timber, the oriel might be a landing at the top of external stairs, built over a small room on the ground floor. It usually had a window, and sometimes a fireplace. In the fourteenth century, oriels expanded into great upper-floor bay windows. An example for an extraordinary purpose was added to Stirling Castle during the siege by Edward I in 1304 in order to provide the queen of Scotland and her ladies with a comfortable observation post.

In the early Middle Ages, when few castles had large permanent garrisons, not only servants but military and administrative personnel slept in towers or in basements, or in the hall, or in lean-to structures; knights performing castle guard slept near their assigned posts. Later, when castles were manned by larger garrisons, often of mercenaries, separate barracks, mess halls, and kitchens were built.

An indispensable feature of the castle of a great lord was the chapel where the lord and his family heard morning mass. In rectangular hall-keeps this was often in the forebuilding, sometimes at basement level, sometimes on the second floor. By the thirteenth century, the chapel was usually close to the hall, convenient to the high table and bed chamber, forming an L with the main building or sometimes projecting opposite the chamber. A popular arrangement was to build the chapel two stories high, with the nave divided horizontally; the family sat in the upper part, reached from their chamber, while the servants occupied the lower part.

Except for the screens and kitchen passages, the domestic quarters of medieval castles contained no internal corridors. Rooms opened into each other, or were joined by spiral

Restormel Castle, Cornwall: Twelfth-century shell keep with domestic buildings and barracks added in thirteenth century around inside of wall, with a central court. Projecting building at right is the chapel.
(Department of the Environment)

staircases which required minimal space and could serve pairs of rooms on several floors. Covered external passageways called pentices joined a chamber to a chapel or to a wardrobe and might have windows, paneling, and even fireplaces.

Water for washing and drinking was available at a central drawing point on each floor. Besides the well, inside or near the keep, there might be a cistern or reservoir on an upper level whose pipes carried water to the floors below. Hand washing was sometimes done at a laver or built-in basin in a recess in the hall entrance, with a projecting trough. Servants filled a tank above, and waste water was carried away by a lead pipe below, inflow and outflow controlled by valves with bronze or copper taps and spouts.

Baths were taken in a wooden tub, protected by a tent or canopy and padded with cloth. In warm weather, the tub was often placed in the garden; in cold weather, in the chamber near the fire. When the lord traveled, the tub accompanied him, along with a bathman who prepared the baths. In some important thirteenth-century castles and palaces there were permanent bathrooms, and in Henry III's palace at Westminster there was even hot and cold running water in the bath house, the hot water supplied by tanks filled from pots heated in a special furnace. Edward II had a tiled floor in his bathroom, with mats to protect his feet from the cold.

The latrine, or "garderobe," an odd euphemism not to be confused with wardrobe, was situated as close to the bed chamber as possible (and was supplemented by the universally used chamber pot). Ideally, the garderobe was sited at the end of a short, right-angled passage in the thickness of the wall, often in a buttress. When the chamber walls were not thick enough for this arrangement, a latrine was corbeled out from the wall over either a moat or river, as in the domestic range at Chepstow, or with a long shaft reaching nearly to the ground. This latter arrangement

ICI FIST DEL EVE VIN:

sometimes proved dangerous in siege, as at Château Gaillard, Richard the Lionhearted's castle on the Seine, where attackers obtained access by climbing up the latrine shaft. As a precaution, the end of the shaft was later protected by a masonry wall. Often several latrines were grouped together into a tower, sometimes in tiers, with a pit below, at the angle of the hall or solar, making them easier to clean. In some castles rainwater from gutters above or from a cistern or diverted kitchen drainage flushed the shaft.

Henry III, traveling from one of his residences to another, sent orders ahead:

> Since the privy chamber . . . in London is situated in an undue and improper place, wherefore it smells badly, we command you on the faith and love by which you are bounden to us that you in no wise omit to cause another privy chamber to be made . . . in such more fitting and proper place that you may select there, even though it should cost a hundred pounds, so that it may be made before the feast of the Translation of St. Edward, before we come thither.

Before a visit to York in 1251 for the marriage of his daughter Margaret to Alexander III of Scotland, the king specified a privy chamber twenty feet long "with a deep pit" to be constructed next to his room in the archbishop's palace.

Hay often served as toilet paper; Jocelin of Brakelond tells how Abbot Samson of Bury St. Edmunds one night dreamed he heard a voice telling him to rise, and woke to find a candle carelessly left by another monk in the privy about to fall into the hay.

In a scene from the story of the Marriage at Cana, servants draw water from a well with a dipping beam. (Trustees of the British Museum. MS. Nero C.iv, f. 17)

By the later thirteenth century, the castle had achieved a considerable degree of comfort, convenience, and privacy. The lord and lady, who had begun by eating and sleeping in the great hall with their household, had gradually withdrawn to their own apartments. Bishop Robert Grosse-teste thought the tendency toward privacy had gone too far and advised the countess of Lincoln: "When not prevented by sickness or fatigue, constrain yourself to eat in the hall before your people, for this shall bring great benefit and honour to you . . . . Forbid dinners and suppers out of the hall and in private rooms, for from this arises waste and no honour to the lord and lady."

A century later, in *Piers Plowman*, William Langland echoed the bishop's warning. Langland blamed the change on technology: the wall fireplace, with its draft chimney, which freed the household from huddling around the central hearth of the old days:

> Woe is in the hall each day in the week.
> There the lord and lady like not to sit.
> Now every rich man eats by himself
> In a private parlor to be rid of poor men,
> Or in a chamber with a chimney
> And leaves the great hall.

IV

The Lady

[The lady of Faiel] entered, a golden circlet on her blonde hair. The castellan saluted her, sighing: "Lady, God give you health, honor and joy." She replied: "And God give you pleasure, peace and health." Then he took her hand and made her sit down near him . . . . He looked at her without saying anything, too moved to speak, and grew pale. The lady saw this and apologized for the absence of her husband. The castellan replied that he loved her and that if she did not have mercy on him, nothing mattered to him. The lady reminded him that she was married and that he must ask her for nothing which would soil the honor of herself or her lord. He replied that nothing would keep him from serving her all his life.

—The Castellan of Coucy

Her hair was golden, with little love-locks; her eyes blue and laughing; her face most dainty to see, with lips more vermeil than ever was rose or cherry in the time of summer heat; her teeth white and small; her breasts so firm that they showed beneath her vesture like two

{ 75 }

rounded nuts; so frail was she about the girdle that your hands could have spanned her, and the daisies that she broke with her feet in passing showed altogether black against her instep and her flesh, so white was the fair young maiden.

—Aucassin and Nicolette

The lady of Faiel and Nicolette were heroines of two popular thirteenth-century romances. Renaut de Coucy's lady, "best, noblest and most intelligent of the land," was worshipped by her lover, who wore her sleeve as a token in battle, composed songs to her, and endured a series of painful trials before at last winning her favor. Beautiful, accomplished, adored, she devoted her life to love—outside the marriage bond. Nicolette, for her part, physically exemplified the medieval feminine ideal—blonde, delicate, fair-skinned, boyish of figure.

Scores of similar ladies dazzled lovers in the outpouring of fiction of the twelfth and thirteenth centuries, but how much they reflect the flesh-and-blood lady of the castle is difficult to say. Little information is available on the personalities and private lives of the women who presided over Chepstow and other castles. One fact, however, is well substantiated: The castle lady customarily was a pawn in the game of politics and economics as played by men.

Although a woman could hold land, inherit it, sell it, or give it away, and plead for it in the law courts, most of a woman's life was spent under the guardianship of a man—of her father until she married, of her husband until she was widowed. If her father died before she married, she was placed under the wardship of her father's lord, who was felt to be legitimately concerned in her marriage because her husband would be his vassal. In the case of an heiress, marriage was a highly profitable transaction—a suitor might pay a large sum for the privilege. But wardship itself was a sought-after prize, because the guardian pocketed the income from the estate until the ward's marriage. Many medieval legal battles were fought over rich wards, and even those not so rich attracted greedy notice. In 1185 Henry II ordered an inventory of all the widows and heirs in the realm with a view to possible royal claims. The age, children, lands, livestock, rents, tools, and other possessions of widows were painstakingly enumerated. A typical entry read:

> Alice de Beaufow, widow of Thomas de Beaufow, is in the gift of the lord king [i.e., in his wardship]. She is twenty and has one son as heir, who is two. Her land in Seaton is worth £5 6s. 8d. with this stock, namely two plows, a hundred sheep, two draught animals, five sows, one boar, and four cows. In the first year in which the land has been in her hand she has received in rent 36s. and 10d. and two pounds of pepper, and apart from the rent her tenants have given her 4s. and three loads of oats.

The wardship of a wealthy three-month-old orphan provoked a spirited resistance by Abbot Samson of Bury St. Edmunds against Henry's son Richard the Lionhearted. In the end the king surrendered to the prelate in return for the gift of some hunting dogs and horses. But the abbot was foiled by the infant's grandfather, who successfully kidnapped her, and Samson finally sold his claim to the wardship to the archbishop of Canterbury for 100 pounds. The little girl survived and appreciated in value, the archbishop in his turn selling the wardship to Thomas de Burgh, brother of the king's chamberlain and future justiciar, for 500 marks (333 pounds).

The daughter of a great lord was typically brought up away from home, in the castle of another noble family, or in a convent, where she might spend her life if she did not marry. Education of girls evidently compared favorably with that of their brothers. The differences in the training of the two sexes were given a jocular exaggeration by the writers of romances, who pictured boys as learning "to feed

a bird, to hawk, to know hunting dogs, to shoot bow and
arrow, to play chess and backgammon," or "fencing,
horsemanship and jousting," whereas girls learned "to work
with needle and shuttle . . . read, write and speak Latin,"
or to "sing songs, tell stories and embroider." Ladies of rank
were patrons of poets and wrote poetry themselves, and
some devoted themselves to learning. Yet, like their husbands, ladies enjoyed hunting and hawking (on their seals
they were often portrayed holding a falcon) and chess.

Girlhood was brief. Women were marriageable at twelve
and usually married by fourteen. Heiresses might be
married in form as young as five and betrothed even
younger, though such unions could be annulled before
consummation. By twenty a woman had a number of
children, and by thirty, if she survived the hazards of
childbirth, she might be widowed and remarried, or a
grandmother.

Whereas personal choice and attraction played a part in
the marriages of peasant girls on the manors (where
marriage commonly followed pregnancy), the marriages of
ladies were too important to be left to predilection. There
were exceptions. King Henry III's sister Eleanor, married to
Chepstow's Earl William Marshal II at the age of nine and
widowed at sixteen, married Simon de Montfort, earl of
Leicester, in 1238 in the king's private chapel at Westminster, with the king giving the bride away. The following
year the king quarreled with De Montfort, who, he
revealed, had "basely and clandestinely defiled" Eleanor
during courtship. "You seduced my sister before marriage,
and when I found it out I gave her to you in marriage,
though against my will, in order to avoid scandal," were the
king's words, reported by Matthew Paris.

There is evidence that many marriages were happy. The
fourteenth-century noble author Geoffrey de la Tour touch-
ingly described his late wife as

both fair and good, who had knowledge of all honor . . . and of fair behavior, and of all good she was the bell and flower; and I delighted so much in her that I made for her love songs, ballads, roundels, virelays, and diverse things in the best wise I could. But death, that on all makes war, took her from me, which has made me many a sorrowful thought and great heaviness. And so it is more than twenty years that I have been for her full of great sorrow. For a true lover's heart never forgets the woman he has truly loved.

Although there was no legal divorce, the taboo against consanguineous unions provided general grounds for annulment suits, especially since it extended to distant cousins, and even relationship by marriage could be invoked. The Church did not always admit such claims. When in 1253 Earl Roger Bigod, lord of Chepstow and grandson of the first William Marshal, repudiated his wife, the daughter of the king of Scotland, because he was allegedly related to her, the Church ruled that he should take her back, and Roger gave in: "Since such is the judgment of the Church, I safely and willingly accede to the marriage, of which I was formerly doubtful and suspicious."

The bride brought a marriage portion and received in return a dower amounting to a third part of her husband's estate, sometimes specific lands named at the church door on her wedding day, which became hers on her husband's

A lady gives her heart to her lover. (Bodleian Library. MS. Bod. 264, f. 59)

death. Even without this formal assignment, a third of his lands was legally hers, and if the heir was slow to turn it over to her, she could bring an action in the royal courts to secure it. The dower was accepted as a fixed charge throughout the feudal age, but was gradually replaced by a settlement made at the time of the marriage.

Once married, a woman was "under the rod" or "under the power" of her husband. She could not "gainsay" him even if he sold land which she had inherited, could not plead in court without him, or make a will without his consent.

Women recovered some of these rights when they became widows. Sometimes a widow even successfully sued to recover land sold by her husband "whom in his lifetime she could not gainsay." But in England before Magna Carta the king could force the widows of his tenants-in-chief to remarry, and if they wished to remain unmarried or to choose their own husbands they had to pay him large fines. Magna Carta limited the king's power in this respect while reiterating that a widow must not marry without the consent of her lord, whether he was the king or one of the king's vassals. Another article of Magna Carta provided that the king's wards, whether widows or maidens, should not be "disparaged"—married to someone of lower rank.

Consent was one of the legal conditions for marriage, and marriages could be annulled on the grounds that they had been contracted against the will of one of the parties. In 1215 King John gave young Lady Margaret, daughter of his chamberlain and widow of the earl of Devon's heir, as a reward to the mercenary captain Falkes de Bréauté. When Falkes was exiled in 1224, Margaret presented herself before the king and the archbishop and asked for an annulment, declaring that she had never consented to the marriage. On her death in 1252, Matthew Paris, characterizing the marriage as "nobility united to meanness, piety to

impiety, beauty to dishonor," quoted a Latin verse someone
had written about the marriage:

Law joined them, love and concord of the bed.
But what kind of law? What kind of love? What kind of concord?
Law out of law, love that was hate, concord that was discord.

The chronicler did not mention the fact that Margaret, who
had been married to Falkes for nine years and had had at
least one child by him, had waited for his downfall to seek
legal redress. Falkes died in Rome in 1226 while petitioning
the Pope to restore his wife and her patrimony to him.

For all her legal disabilities, the lady played a serious,
sometimes leading role in the life of the castle. When the
lord was away at court, war, Crusade, or pilgrimage, she
ran the estate, directing the staff and making the financial
and legal decisions. The ease with which castle ladies took
over such functions indicates a familiarity implying at least
a degree of partnership when the lord was at home. Besides
helping to supervise the household staff and the ladies who
acted as nurses for her children, the lord's wife took charge
of the reception and entertainment of officials, knights,
prelates, and other castle visitors. Bishop Robert Grosseteste
advised the countess of Lincoln to deal with her guests
"quickly, courteously and with good cheer," and to see that
they were "courteously addressed, lodged and served."

Inferior legal status did not reduce women to voiceless
shadows. Contemporary satirists in fact pictured women as
quarrelsome and pugnacious. In one of his sermons, the
famous Paris preacher Jacques de Vitry told the story of the
man with a wife

> so contrary that she always did the reverse of what he
> commanded, and received in a surly manner the guests
> whom he often asked to dinner. One day he invited several to
> dine with him, and had the tables set in the garden near a
> stream. His wife sat with her back to the water, at some

distance from the table, and regarded the guests with an
unfriendly face. Her husband said: "Be cheerful to our
guests, and draw nearer the table." She on the contrary
pushed her chair farther from the table and nearer the edge
of the stream at her back. Her husband, noticing this, said
angrily: "Draw near the table." She pushed her chair
violently back and fell into the river and was drowned. Her
husband jumped in a boat and began to seek his wife with a
long pole, but up the stream. When his neighbors asked him
why he looked for his wife up the stream instead of below as
he should, he answered: "Do you not know that my wife
always did what was contrary and never walked in the
straight way? I verily believe that she has gone up against the
current and not down with it like other people."

An incident of 1252 described by Matthew Paris fur-
nishes a picture of the medieval lady as a person capable of
self-assertion even against so daunting an opponent as the
king. Isabella, countess of Arundel, visited King Henry III
to protest his claim of a wardship of which he owned a small
portion, but which belonged mainly to her. The countess,
"although a woman" (in Matthew Paris' aside), demanded,
"Why, my lord king, do you avert your face from justice?
One cannot now obtain what is right and just at your court.
You are appointed a mediator between the Lord and us,
but you do not govern well either yourself or us . . .
moreover, without fear or shame, you oppress the nobles of
the kingdom in divers ways." The king replied ironically,
"What is this, my lady countess? Have the nobles of
England . . . given you a charter to be their spokeswoman
and advocate, as you are so eloquent?" The countess
answered, "By no means, my lord, have the nobles of your
kingdom given me a charter, but you have given me that
charter [Magna Carta], which your father granted to me,
and which you agreed and swore to observe faithfully and
to keep inviolate . . . I, although a woman, and all of us,
your natural and faithful subjects, appeal against you
before the tribunal of the awful judge of all; and heaven

and earth will be our witnesses, since you treat us with injustice, though we are innocent of crime against you—and may the Lord, the God of vengeance, avenge me." The king, according to Matthew, was silenced by this speech, "and the countess, without obtaining, or even asking for permission, returned home."

Notwithstanding feudal law, a woman occasionally even arranged her own marriage. Isabelle of Angoulême, widow of King John, found an opportunity to make an advantageous (or at any rate congenial) second marriage, and seized it, in the process displacing her own ten-year-old daughter Joan, who had been betrothed to the man in question for six years. Isabelle wrote home to her "dearest son," King Henry III, from Angoulême, whither she had gone to take up the reins of government of the county:

> We hereby notify you that, the Count of La Marche [the bridegroom's father, who had died on Crusade] . . . having departed this life, the lord Hugh de Lusignan is left, as it were, alone and without heir . . . and his friends would not allow our daughter to be united with him in lawful marriage because of her tender age, but advise him to seek an heir speedily, and it is proposed that he should take a wife in France. If that were to happen, all your lands in Poitou and Gascony and ours too would be lost. Seeing the great danger that might result if such a union took place, and getting no advice from your councillors . . . we have therefore taken the said Hugh, Count of La Marche, as our lord and husband; and let God be our witness that we have done this more for your welfare than our own. Wherefore we ask you, as our dear son . . . since this may yield greatest benefit to you and yours, that you restore to us what is ours by right, namely Niort, Exeter, and Rockingham, and the 3,500 marks which your father, our late husband, bequeathed us.

Isabelle's dowry and inheritance were not forthcoming, however, Henry refusing to relinquish them until Joan, in custody in La Marche, was back in England, and Isabelle refusing to give up Joan until she had the lands and money. Under pressure from the Pope, Isabelle and Hugh at last yielded up Joan, who then married King Alexander of Scotland. But Henry, Isabelle, and Hugh continued to bicker over the dowry for many years.

Another spirited lady was described by the chronicler Ordericus Vitalis.

> The faculties of [William] count of Évreux [d. 1118] were naturally somewhat feeble as well as being reduced by old age, and trusting perhaps more than was proper to his wife's abilities, he left the administration of his county [of Évreux] completely in her hands. The Countess [Helvise] was notable for her wit and beauty. She was one of the tallest women in all Évreux and of very high birth . . . . Ignoring the counsels of her husband's barons, she chose instead to follow her own ideas and ambition. Often inspiring audacious measures in political affairs, she readily engaged in rash enterprises.

Many medieval ladies showed political capacity of a high order. Countess Matilda of Tuscany presided over one of the most important feudal states in eleventh-century Italy, decisively intervened on the side of the Pope against Emperor Henry IV in the greatest political struggle of her day, and made her castle of Canossa a byword in Western languages. Blanche of Castile ruled France for a quarter of the thirteenth century. In England the wives of William the Conqueror, Henry I, and Henry II all served as regents during their husbands' absences.

Although at a disadvantage in a military society, women not only defended their castles in sieges but actually led armies in battles. Long before Joan of Arc, women put on armor and rode to war. William the Conqueror's granddaughter Matilda, called the Empress Matilda because of her earlier marriage to the German emperor Henry V, led her army in person against her cousin Stephen of Blois in England's twelfth-century civil war. Momentarily victorious, Matilda, according to the hostile chronicler of the *Gesta Stephani* ("Deeds of Stephen"), "at once put on an extremely arrogant demeanor, instead of the modest gait and bearing proper to a gentle woman, and began to walk and speak and do all things more stiffly and more haughtily than she had been wont, . . . began to be arbitrary, or rather headstrong, in all that she did." The *Gesta Stephani* went on to describe Matilda's behavior at Winchester when the king of Scotland, the bishop of Winchester, and her brother, the earl of Gloucester, "the chief men of the whole kingdom" and part of her permanent retinue, came before her with bended knee to make a request. Instead of rising respectfully to greet them and agreeing to what they asked, she brusquely dismissed them and refused to listen to their advice. Later she advanced upon London with a large army, and when the citizens welcomed her, according to the chronicler, replied by sending for the richest men and demanding "a huge sum of money, not with unassuming gentleness, but with a voice of authority." Upon their protesting, she lost her temper.

Later, her fortune changing, Matilda was besieged in Oxford Castle. She again showed mettle,

> [leaving] the castle by night, with three knights of ripe judgment to accompany her, and went about six miles on foot, by very great exertions on the part of herself and her companions, through the snow and ice (for all the ground was white with an extremely heavy fall of snow, and there was a very thick crust of ice on the water). What was the evident sign of a miracle, she crossed dry-footed, without wetting her clothes at all, the very waters that had risen above the heads of the king [Stephen] and his men when they were going over to storm the town, and through the king's pickets, which everywhere were breaking the silence of the night with the blaring of trumpeters or the cries of men shouting loudly, without anyone at all knowing except her companions.

At one point in the struggle, the Empress Matilda found herself pitted against another Matilda, Stephen's wife, "a woman of subtlety and a man's resolution," who led troops in an attack on London, ordering them to "rage most furiously around the city with plunder and arson, violence and the sword."

A thirteenth-century lady who played a military role was Dame Nicolaa de la Haye, widow of the sheriff of Lincoln, a "vigorous old lady," in the words of a chronicler, who commanded the royalist stronghold of Lincoln Castle against the forces of Prince Louis of France and the rebel English barons at the time of King John's death, holding out against every assault until William Marshal arrived with relief forces.

One of the greatest of all examples of hardihood and independence was the Empress Matilda's daughter-in-law, Eleanor, heiress to the vast province of Aquitaine in southwestern France. Eleanor's first marriage, to Louis VII of France, was terminated by her affair with Raymond of Antioch in the Holy Land, but far from retiring to a convent after the scandal, Eleanor married Matilda's son, who two years later gained the English throne as Henry II. Eleanor meddled actively in politics, encouraging her sons in rebellions against their father until exasperated Henry imprisoned her in Salisbury Castle. (Chepstow's William Marshal was sent in 1183 to tell her that Henry had released her.) After Henry's death she traveled from city to city and castle to castle in England and France, holding court, and at the age of eighty she played a decisive role in the struggle for the English throne between her grandson Arthur and her son John.

Eleanor's native French province, Aquitaine, was the birthplace of the poetry of the troubadours, founders of the Western poetic tradition. Eleanor's grandfather, Count William IX of Aquitaine, was the earliest troubadour whose work has survived, and Eleanor is sometimes credited with the introduction of troubadour verse into northern France and England. Eleanor's daughter by her first marriage, Marie de Champagne, was also a patroness of poets, notably the celebrated Chrétien de Troyes, creator of the Lancelot-Guinevere romance. At Marie's court in Troyes (or at the court of France) a work was formulated that had immense influence in aristocratic circles: *De Amore* ("On Love"), written by Andreas Capellanus ("André the Chaplain"), borrowing freely from Ovid. The treatise supplies an insight into the manners, morals, conversation, and thought of the noble ladies of the High Middle Ages, revealing a sophistication and wit at variance both with the image of pampered sex object of the romances and with the disfranchised pawn of the legal system.

The thesis of *De Amore* is summed up in a letter purported to be written by Countess Marie to Andreas in response to the question of whether true love could have any place in marriage:

> We declare and we hold as firmly established that love cannot exert its powers between two people who are married to each other. For lovers give each other everything freely, under no compulsion or necessity, but married people are in duty bound to give in to each other's desires and deny themselves to each other in nothing.
>
> Besides, how does it increase a husband's honor if after the manner of lovers he enjoys the embraces of his wife, since the worth of character of neither can be increased thereby, and they seem to have nothing more than they already had a right to?
>
> And we say the same thing for still another reason, which is that a precept of love tells us that no woman, even if she is married, can be crowned with the reward of the King of Love unless she is seen to be enlisted in the service of Love himself outside the bonds of wedlock. But another rule of Love teaches that no one can be in love with two men. Rightly, therefore, Love cannot acknowledge any rights of his between husband and wife.

Lovers kneel before Eros, who aims an arrow at one of them. (Trinity College, Cambridge. MS. B.11.22)

But there is still another argument that seems to stand in the way of this, which is that between them there can be no true jealousy, and without it true love may not exist, according to the rule of Love himself, which says, "He who is not jealous cannot love."

A chapter of *De Amore* cited "love cases" which were supposed to have been tried in "courts of love" before ladies of Eleanor's and Marie's courts and those of other noble ladies—assemblages now believed to be no more than an elegant fiction:

A certain lady had a proper enough lover, but was afterward, through no fault of her own, married to an honorable man, and she avoided her lover and denied him his usual solaces. But Lady Ermengarde of Narbonne demonstrated the lady's bad character in these words: "The later contracting of a marital union does not properly exclude an early love except in cases where the woman gives up love entirely and is determined by no means to love any more. . . ."

A certain woman had been married, but was now separated from her husband by a divorce, and her former husband sought eagerly for her love. In this case the lady replied: "If any two people have been married and afterward separate in any way, we consider love between them wholly wicked. . . ."

A certain knight was in love with a woman who had given her love to another man, but he got from her this much hope of her love—that if it should ever happen that she lost the love of her beloved, then without a doubt her love would go to this man. A little while after this the woman married her lover. The other knight then demanded that she give him the fruit of the hope she had granted him, but this she absolutely refused to do, saying that she had not lost the love of her lover. In this affair the Queen gave her decision as follows: "We dare not oppose the opinion of the Countess of Champagne, who ruled that love can exert no power between husband and wife. Therefore we recommend that the lady should grant the love she has promised. . . ."

The Countess of Champagne was also asked what gifts it was proper for ladies to accept from their lovers. To the man who asked this the Countess replied, "A woman who loves may freely accept from her lover the following: a handkerchief, a fillet for the hair, a wreath of gold or silver, a breastpin, a mirror, a girdle, a purse, a tassel, a comb, sleeves, gloves, a ring, a compact, a picture, a wash basin, little dishes, trays, a flag as a souvenir . . . any little gift which may be useful for the care of the person or pleasing to look at or which may call the lover to her mind, if it is clear that in accepting the gift she is free from all avarice.

"But . . . if a woman receives a ring from her lover as a pledge of love, she ought to put it on her left hand and on her little finger, and she should always keep the stone hidden on the inside of her hand; this is because the left hand is usually kept freer from dishonesty and shameful contacts, and a man's life and death are said to reside more in his little finger than in the others, and because all lovers are bound to keep their lover secret. Likewise, if they correspond with each other by letter they should refrain from signing their own names. Furthermore, if the lovers should for any reason come before a court of ladies, the identity of the lovers should never be revealed to the judges, but the case should be presented anonymously. And they ought not to seal their letters to each other with their own seals unless they happen to have secret seals known only to themselves and their confidants. In this way their love will always be retained unimpaired."

If "courtly love" (a phrase coined in much later times) was the medieval literary ideal, in practice a firmly masculine double standard prevailed toward adultery. The Church condemned it in both sexes, but commonly kings, earls, barons, and knights had mistresses, and illegitimate children abounded (Henry I had twenty-odd, John five known bastards). Adultery in women was a different matter, and an erring wife was often disgraced and repudiated, her lover mutilated or killed. The issue was not morality but masculine honor. Adultery with the lord's wife was regarded as treason. In the reign of Philip the Fair of France two nobles accused of adultery with the wives of the king's sons were castrated, dragged behind horses to the gallows, and hanged as "not only adulterers, but the vilest traitors to their lords."

The fine points of matters of honor (as well as the fact that the honor in question was exclusively masculine) are illustrated by two cases recorded by Matthew Paris. A knight named Godfrey de Millers entered the house of another knight "for the purpose of lying with his daughter" but was seized, with the connivance of the girl herself, "who was afraid of being thought a married man's mistress," and was beaten and castrated. The perpetrators of this deed, including the girl's father, were punished by exile and the seizure of their property. Ambiguous though the evidence was—the girl may well have simply been defending herself against attack—Matthew Paris unhesitatingly pronounced her a "harlot" and "adultress" and the punishment of the knight "a deed of enormous cruelty . . . an inhuman and merciless crime." At about the same time "a certain handsome clerk, the rector of a rich church," who distinguished himself by surpassing all the neighboring knights by the lavishness of his hospitality and entertainment—a universally admired trait in aristocratic circles—was similarly treated for a similar malfeasance. The king, like Matthew Paris, deeply grieved at the cleric's misfortune, ordered it to be proclaimed as law that no one should be castrated for adultery except by a cuckolded husband, whose honor, unlike that of the lady's father, her family, or the lady herself, was sacred.

The man who made a conquest, on the other hand, might boast of it—as did Eleanor of Aquitaine's grandfather William IX when he versified about disguising himself as a deaf-mute and visiting the wives of "Lords Guarin and Bernard" (whether these were the names of real personages is not known). After testing him and assuring themselves that he in truth was "dumb as a stone,"

> Then Ann to Lady Eleanor said:
> "He *is* mute, plain as eyes in your head;
> Sister, get ready for bath and bed
>   And dalliance gay."
> Eight days thereafter in that furnace
>   I had to stay.
>
> How much I tupped them you shall hear:
> A hundred eighty-eight times or near,
> So that I almost stripped my gear
>   And broke my equipment;
> I never could list the ills I got—
>   Too big a shipment.

Medieval ideas were far from the Victorian notion that nice women did not enjoy sex. Physiologically, men and women were considered sexual equals—in fact, as in William IX's verses, women were commonly credited with stronger sexual feelings than men. In the fabliaux and in the satiric writings of medieval moralists women were constantly portrayed as lusty and even insatiable. The

author of the thirteenth-century *Lamentations of Matthew*
complained that his wife claimed her conjugal rights with
energy, and "if I don't give them to her because I don't
have my old vigor, she pulls my hair."

An excerpt from a commentary on Aristotle by the
thirteenth-century German scholar Albertus Magnus,
widely circulated under the title *On the Secrets of Women*,
asked the question, Was pleasure in intercourse greater in
men than in women? The answer was no. In the first place,
according to the sages, since matter desires to take on form,
a woman, an imperfect human being, desires to come
together with a man, because the imperfect naturally
desires to be perfected. Therefore the greater pleasure and
appetite belonged to the woman. In the second place,
orgasm was the indication of the emission of the female seed
in intercourse. Double pleasure was better than single
pleasure, and while in men pleasure came from the emission
of seed, in women pleasure came from both emission and
reception. Consequently, any woman who conceived was
believed to have taken pleasure in intercourse, and judges
denied suit for rape if a woman became pregnant from the
assault. Another theory of Albertus, also taken from Aristotle, stated that the female seed, or *menstruum,* gradually
collected in the womb, increasing sexual desire as it
accumulated. Menstruation, seen as the equivalent of a
man's ejaculation, provided periodic relief. Therefore,
though men's pleasure might be more intensive, women's
was more extensive. During pregnancy, when the *menstruum*
was retained to form and nourish the fetus, a woman was
thought to be at the peak of her sexual desire. The sexual
attitudes set forth by Albertus were also an expression of a
cleric's contempt for women; the woman's desire was
greater not merely physiologically, but because of the
weakness of her judgment, and because of her imperfection,
the inferior's desire for the superior.

The conventions of chivalry directed that, in the words of

the thirteenth-century *Roman de la Rose*, men should "do honor to ladies. . . . Serve ladies and maidens if you would be honored by all." Men were to be courteous, witty, accomplished, to speak gently, to "do nothing to displease" a lady—yet in practice a lord might strike or beat his wife. Geoffrey de La Tour tells of a man breaking his wife's nose because she talked back to him before strangers, "and all her life she had her nose crooked, which spoiled and disfigured her visage so that she could not for shame show it, it was so foully blemished."

Courtesy, in any case, did not mean an improvement in women's status; on the contrary, it emphasized woman's role as an object. A dialogue between a knight and lady in *De Amore* told of a lady, loved by two suitors, who "divided the solaces of love" into two parts and let them choose either the upper or the lower half of her; the question to be debated was which suitor had chosen the better part. The knight contended that the solaces of the upper part were superior, since they were not those of the brute beasts, and since one never tired of practicing them, whereas "the delight of the lower part quickly palls upon those who practice it, and it makes them repent of what they have done." The lady disagreed: "Whatever lovers do has as its only object the obtaining of the solaces of the lower part, for there is fulfilled the whole effect of love, at which all lovers chiefly aim and without which they think they have nothing more than certain preludes to love." In *De Amore* the question was resolved in favor of the knight, but it was adjudged differently in another work, the French *Lai du Lecheoir* ("Lay of the Lecher"): Eight ladies in a Breton court, "wise and learned," discussed the question of knights' motives for their tournaments, jousts, and adventures:

> Why are they good knights?
> Why do they love tournaments? . . .
> Why do they dress in new clothes?
> Why do they send us their jewels,

Their treasures and their rings?
Why are they frank and debonair?
Why do they refrain from doing evil?
Why do they like gallantry . . . ?

The answer is given by the poet in a series of plays on the French word *con*, the earthy designation for the center of the "solaces of the lower part."

Whatever the effect on the lady of the castle, the ideas of chivalry and courtly love had their influence for good or ill on a later age, in much of modern etiquette, and above all in the concept of romantic love.

V

The Household

BESIDES THE LORD, HIS LADY, AND THEIR CHILDREN, the household of a castle consisted of a staff that varied in size with the wealth of the lord, but that usually comprehended two main divisions. The military personnel, or *mesnie,* included household knights and knights from outside performing castle-guard duty, squires, men-at-arms, a porter who kept the outer door of the castle, and watchmen. The ministerial and domestic staff, headed by the steward, or seneschal, administered the estate, handled routine financial and legal matters, and directed the servants.

Out of a natural division of duties by departments of the house grew the principal offices of the castle. The steward was at first the servant in charge of the great hall; the chaplain or chancellor was in charge of the chapel or chancel (the altar area of a church); the chamberlain was responsible for the great chamber; the keeper of the wardrobe, for clothing; the butler (or bottler), for the buttery, where beverages were kept, in butts or bottles; the usher, for the door of the hall; the cook, for the kitchen; and the marshal, for the stables. Some of these offices expanded in the course of time to entail larger duties: The steward became the manager of the estate; sometimes the chamberlain, sometimes the wardrobe keeper became the treasurer; the chaplain and his assistants became a secretarial department.

In royal households, the duties gradually decayed into honorific rituals. The biographer of William Marshal tells how on Christmas Day in Caen, just before the feast, a servant prepared to pour water for Henry II and his sons to wash their hands when William Marshal's sponsor, the Norman baron William of Tancarville, burst into the room, seized basins and executed the function which was his by right as hereditary chamberlain of Normandy. Matthew Paris described the ceremonies at the wedding of Henry III, in which the king's great barons performed the menial tasks prescribed by their offices:

> The grand marshal of England, the earl of Pembroke [William Marshal's son Gilbert] carried a wand before the king and cleared the way before him both in the church and in the banquet hall, and arranged the banquet and the guests at table . . . . The earl of Leicester supplied the king with water in basins to wash before his meal, the Earl Warenne performed the duty of king's cupbearer, supplying the place of the earl of Arundel because the latter was a youth and not as yet made a belted knight . . . . The justiciar of the forests arranged the drinking cups on the table at the king's right hand . . . .

Under the household officials a large staff of servants operated. In 1265 the king's sister Eleanor de Montfort, countess of Leicester, had more than sixty, while in the 1270s the household of Bogo de Clare, an ecclesiastical kinsman of the Chepstow lords whose accounts have

survived, included two knights, "numerous" squires, thir-
teen grooms, two pages, a cook, a doctor, and many clerks
and lesser servants.

The most important member of the castle staff was the
steward. In the twelfth century the steward commonly
supervised both the lord's estates and his household, but by
the thirteenth century there were often two stewards, one in
charge of the estates, the other in charge of the domestic
routine. The estates steward, frequently a knight, held the
lord's courts, headed the council of knights and officials that
advised the lord, supervised local officials, and sometimes
represented the lord at the king's court or acted as his
deputy. He was highly paid, furnished with fine robes
trimmed with fur, and sometimes had a house of his own.
Simon de Montfort's steward, Richard of Havering, held
one-fourth of a knight's fee from his lord, together with
other lands and rents, including a parcel for which the
annual rent was a symbolic single rose. During the great
baronial rebellion led by Simon in 1265 his trusted steward
was given charge of Wallingford Castle.

With the aid of auditors, the steward kept the accounts of
the lord's lands and fiefs, listing the revenues, acreage,
produce, and livestock on each manor, the taxes and other
charges paid, the money rents, and the profits from his law
courts.

A thirteenth-century manual on estate administration
called *Seneschaucie* ("Stewardship") described the require-
ments for the steward, or seneschal:

> The seneschal of lands ought to be prudent and faithful
> and profitable, and he ought to know the law of the realm, to
> protect his lord's business and to instruct and give assurance
> to the bailiffs who are beneath him in their difficulties. He
> ought two or three times a year to make his rounds and visit
> the manors of his stewardship, and then he ought to inquire
> about the rents, services, and customs . . . and about
> franchises of courts, lands, woods, meadows, pastures, waters,

mills, and other things which belong to the manor . . . .

The seneschal ought at first coming to the manors to cause all the demesne lands of each to be measured by true men . . . to see and inquire how they are tilled, and in what crops they are, and how the cart-horses and cattle, oxen, cows, sheep and swine are kept and improved . . . . The seneschal ought to see that each manor is properly stocked, and if there be overcharge on any manor more than the pasture can bear, let the overcharge be moved to another manor where there is less stock. And if the lord be in want of money to pay the debts due, or to make a purchase at a particular term, the seneschal ought before the term, and before the time that need arises, to look to the manors from which he can have money at the greatest advantage and smallest loss . . . .

The seneschal ought, on coming to the manors, to inquire how the bailiff bears himself within and without, what care he takes, what improvement he makes, and what increase and profit there is in the manor in his office, because of his being there. And also of . . . all other offices . . . . He ought to remove all those that are not necessary for the lord, and all the servants who do nothing . . . .

The seneschal ought, on his coming to the manors, to inquire about wrong-doings and trespasses done in parks, ponds, warrens, rabbit runs, and dove-houses, and of all other things which are done to the loss of the lord in his office.

A picture of a steward at work is given by the letters of Simon of Senlis, steward of the bishop of Chichester, who reported to his lord in 1226:

Know, my lord, that William de St. John is not in Sussex, wherefore I cannot at present carry through the business which you enjoined upon me, but as soon as he comes into Sussex, I will work as hard as I can to dispatch and complete it in accordance with your honor. I sent to you 85 ells of cloth bought for distribution for the use of the poor. As regards the old wine which is in your cellar at Chichester, I cannot sell to your advantage because of the over-great abundance of new wine in the town of Chichester. Further, my lord, know that

a certain burgess of Chichester holds one croft which belongs
to the garden given to you by our lord the king, for which he
pays two shillings a year, which the sheriff of Sussex demands
from him. Wherefore, since the land belongs to the said
garden, and was removed from it in ancient times, please
give me your advice about the said rent. I am having marling
[fertilizing with clay containing carbonate of lime] properly
done in your manor of Selsey, and by this time five acres
have been marled . . . .

Later he wrote:

To Richard, whom Thomas of Cirencester sent to you, I have
committed the keeping of the manor of Preston, since, as I
think, he understands the care of sheep, and I will see that
your woods at Chichester are meanwhile well treated, by the
grace of God, and are brought to their proper state; also I
wish your excellency to know that Master R., your official,
and I shall be at Aldingbourne on the Sunday after St.
Faith's day, there to make the division between my lord of
Canterbury and you. And if it please you, your long-cart can
easily come to Aldingbourne on that day, so that I can send
to you in London, should you so wish, the game taken in
your parks and other things, and also the cloth bought for the
use of the poor, as much as you wish, and of which I bought
300 ells at Winchester Fair. For at present I cannot send
these by your little carts on the manors because sowing time
is at hand. Among other things, know that the crops in your
manors have been harvested safely and profitably and to
your advantage and placed in your barns.

And again:

Know, dearest lord, that I have been to London, where I
labored with all my might and took care that you should
there have . . . wood for burning, brewing and repairs.
Thanks be to God, all your affairs, both at West Mulne and
elsewhere, go duly and prosperously. Also I have taken care
that you should have what I judge to be a sufficient quantity
of lambs' wool for your household against the winter . . . .
Speak also with Robert of Lexington about having beef for

your larder in London . . . . If you think it wise, my lord, I beg that part of the old corn from West Mulne shall be ground and sent to London against your coming . . . .

In other letters Simon arranged for the purchase of iron and its transport to Gloucester and then to Winchester; advised his lord to think of getting his sheep from the abbey of Vaudey in Yorkshire and sending them down to his Sussex manors; reported on the vicar of Mundeham's two wives, on a dilatory agent, on the servant of one of the manors whom he wished to promote.

The household steward kept the accounts of the daily expenditures of the castle—sometimes, in a great household, separate accounts for the lord and the lady, and in the royal household even one for the children. Every night, either in person or through a deputy appointed by the lord, the steward went over expenses with the cook, the butler, the pantler (the servant in charge of the pantry, i.e., "bread-ery"), and the marshal, and listed supplies received—meat, fish, grain. The meat was cut up in his presence and enumerated as it was delivered to the cook; the steward had

Food preparation, from the Luttrell Psalter. On the left, meat is boiled in cauldrons, while the cook holds a colander-like spoon and a meat hook. Center, another cook cuts up meat. On the right, a third grinds food in a huge mortar. (Trustees of the British Museum. MS. Add. 42130, f. 207)

to know how many loaves could be made from a quarter of wheat, and see that the baker delivered that number to the pantler.

Household accounts were kept from Michaelmas (September 29) to Michaelmas, and they listed, usually in the same order, the amount of grain or bread, the wine and beer, the kitchen supplies, the stable supplies, the number of horses, the amount of hay and oats, and the manor which furnished them. Guests were also listed. They were not always welcome to the household staff. The accounts of Prince Edward (later Edward II) in June 1293 recorded: "There came to dinner John of Brabant [Prince Edward's brother-in-law], with 30 horses and 24 valets, and the two sons of the Lord Edmund [younger brother of King Edward I], and they stay at our expenses in all things in hay, oats and wages." For four days afterward the accounts laconically reported: "Morantur [They remain]." Finally the entry: "They remain until now, and this is the onerous day"—the guests, with some foreigners, went to the jousts at Fulham, and the household had to provide a sumptuous entertainment.

A rare insight into the domestic economy of the thirteenth-century castle is provided by the accounts of Eleanor de Montfort, the earliest such accounts preserved. For a typical week (in May 1265), they give minute particulars of the household's subsistence. (To give an idea of monetary values, the usual daily wage of a skilled craftsman in the thirteenth century was about 4½ pence—there were 12 pence in a shilling, 20 shillings in a pound.)

> On Sunday, for the Countess and lord Simon de Montfort, and the aforesaid persons [of her household]: bread, 1½ quarters, wine, 4 sextaries; beer, already reckoned. *Kitchen.* Sheep from Everley, 6, also for 1 ox and 3 calves and 8 lbs. of fat, 12s. 2d.; 6 dozen fowls 3s.; also eggs 20d. flour 6d. Bread for the kitchen 3d. Geese 10, already reckoned. *Marshalcy* [stable]. Hay for 50 horses. Oats, 3 quarters and a half.
>
> Sum 17s. 7d.

For the poor, for 15 days, 1 quarter 1 bushel [of bread]. Beer, 34 gallons. Also for the hounds for 15 days, 5 quarters 5 bushels [of bread]. Also for the poor, on Sunday 120 herrings. Paid for preparing 27 quarters of malt wheat from grain at Odiham [Castle], 2s. 3d. Also for the laundry from Christmas, 15d. Also for yeast, 6½d. For the carriage of 3 pipes of wine from Staines to Odiham by Seman, 13s. 6d.; and that wine came from the Earl's household at London.

Sum 17s. 6½d.

On the following Monday, for the Countess and the aforesaid persons, dining at Odiham and leaving late for Portchester [Castle], bread, 1 quarter, 2 bushels of grain; wine, 4½ sextaries; beer already reckoned. *Kitchen.* Meat, already reckoned, eggs, 15d., fowls already reckoned. *Marshalcy.* Smithy, 2d. For one horse placed at the disposal of Dobbe the Parker to guide the Countess, 10d.

Sum 27d.

Tuesday and Wednesday, the household was paid for by lord Simon de Montfort at Portchester.

On the Thursday following, for the Countess, at Portchester, R. de Bruce and A. de Montfort being present, with their household, and lord Simon's servants, and the garrison of the castle; bread bought, 8s., and also ½ a quarter received from a servant from Chawton; wine, from stock. *Kitchen.* Meat bought, 2s. 5d., 6 sheep from a servant from Chawton, and 1 cured hog from the stock of the castle. Eggs, 400, 18d. Salt, 3½d. *Marshalcy.* Hay for 45 horses, of which the Countess had 24, the lord Simon and his household 9, Amaury 8, the parson of Kemsing 3, from the castle stock. Oats, 1 quarter received from the servant from Chawton and 2 quarters bought, 5s. Food for the fowls, 14d.

Sum 18s. 4½d.

On the Friday following, for the Countess and the aforesaid persons, bread 6s. 2d., bought, and also 1 quarter from Chawton. Wine from stock, 8 sextaries good and 10½ sextaries of another sort. *Kitchen.* Mackerel, 21d. Fat, 8d. Mullet and bar, 15d. Flounders, 7d. Eggs, 9d. Meal, 13d. Earthen pots, 3d. Salt, 3½d. Capers, 3½d. *Marshalcy.* Hay for 48 horses, of which the lord Simon had 12, 12d. Oats, 3 qrs., 1 bushel, of which 1 quarter was bought, and cost 2s. 6d. For gathering grass for 3 nights, 2d.

Sum 16s. 9d.

On the Saturday following, for the Countess and the aforesaid persons, J. de Katerington and others; bread 1½ quarters, from the servant from Chawton; wine, 16 sextaries, of which 9 were of good wine. Pots and cups, 6½d. *Kitchen.* Fish, 4s. 7d., eggs, 2s. 4d., cheese for tarts, 10d. For 4 mortars bought, 17d. For vinegar and mustard, 5d. Porterage, 5d. *Marshalcy.* Grass, bought in bulk, 13s. 1d. Oats for 52 horses, of which the lord Simon had 12, 2½ quarters, from the servant from Chawton. For carrying two cartloads of grass, 7½d.

Sum 24s. 3½d.

Administration of an estate required specialized training —in letter-writing, legal procedure, the preparation of documents, and accounting. Beginning in the reign of Henry III, a regular course in estate management was taught by masters in the town of Oxford. The course, which seems to have taken from six months to a year, prepared the young man who had the opportunity of entering the employ of a lord for his practical apprenticeship.

It was a career worth entering. The steward's legitimate perquisites were excellent and were reputed to be frequently augmented by less legitimate ones. A fourteenth-century book of manners declared of stewards, "Few are true, but many are false," and the moralist Robert Mannyng commented that dishonest stewards and other servants

> . . . do much wrong in many things;
> Therefore shall they and their counsel
> Go to hell, both top and tail.

Henry III's butler, a knight named Poyntz Piper, enriched himself as a member of the king's household "by
unlawful as well as lawful means," according to Matthew
Paris, progressing from the ownership of a few acres of land
to "having the wealth of an earl." Poyntz's manors included
one at Tedington, where he built a palace, chapel, and
other fine stone buildings with lead roofs and established
orchards and warrens. Matthew recorded with satisfaction
in 1251 that Poyntz had "gone the way of all flesh," and
that his widow had married "a brave and handsome
knight," who fell heir to all of the estates acquired by the
deceased.

The pantry, larder, buttery, and kitchen had their own
staffs, including dispensers, cupbearers, fruiterers, a slaugh-
terer, a baker, a brewer, a man to look after the tablecloths,
a wafer maker, a candle maker, a sauce cook, and a
poulterer, each with boy helpers. The chamberlain employed a cofferer, who was responsible for the chests that
contained money and plate—silver cups, saucers, spoons.
The keeper of the wardrobe employed tailors to make the
robes of the lord and the livery of his retainers. A laundress
washed the clothes, sheets, tablecloths, and towels (Bogo de
Clare's laundress also washed his hair).

The marshal's stable staff included grooms, smiths,
carters, and clerks. Their duties included transporting
household goods, delivering purchases made at the fairs or
from London merchants, and arranging for the supply of
bran, oats, and hay for the horses, and sometimes procuring
horseshoes and nails. The marshal and his clerks bought
other supplies (carts, sacks, and trunks for the pack horses),
paid the grooms, and checked the state of horses and carts.
Horses too old for service were given to the poor. Carts were
repaired, their iron fittings replaced, axles greased, harness
renewed.

Full-time messengers were indispensable to a great lord

whose holdings were scattered over a large area. They transported receipts and commodities as well as letters, and ranked in status and pay between the grooms below them and the squires and men-at-arms above them. Besides pay they were provided with robes and shoes every year. Messengers encountered an unusual occupational hazard; Matthew Paris reported that Walter de Clifford, a Welsh baron, was convicted in 1250 of having "in contempt of the king violently and improperly treated his messenger, who bore his royal letters, and of having forced him to eat the same, with the seal." Walter was fined the large sum of 1,000 marks (£667). Later Bogo de Clare's officials similarly treated an emissary of the archbishop of Canterbury, who arrived at Bogo's London house with a citation to serve on the noble prelate. They "by force and against his will made him eat the letters and the appended seals, imprisoned him there, beat and maltreated him." Injury to the messenger was assessed at £20, and damages for contempt of the Church and the king at £1,000, but Bogo succeeded in evading payment.

Another essential department of the lord's household was the office of the chaplain (or chancellor in a very large household). Besides presiding at mass, the chaplain kept the lord's seal and wrote his business and personal letters in Latin or French. His clerk took charge of the vessels and vestments for mass, and when the household traveled was responsible for the transport of the portable altar, a wooden table with a stone center to hold relics. Other clerks assisted with the accounts, ran errands, and made purchases.

An important member of the chaplain's department was the almoner, who had charge of offerings to the poor. The almoner gathered the leftovers from the table and saw that they were distributed among the poor and not pilfered by the servants and grooms. A thirteenth-century manual was emphatic that the king's almoner ought to visit for charity's sake the sick, the lepers, the captive, the poor, the widows and others in want and the wanderers in the countryside, and to receive discarded horses, clothing, money and other gifts, bestowed in alms, and to distribute them faithfully. He ought also by frequent exhortations to spur the king to liberal almsgiving, especially on saints' days, and to implore him not to bestow his robes, which are of great price, upon players, flatterers, fawners, talebearers, or minstrels, but to command them to be used to augment his almsgiving.

Countess Eleanor de Montfort's almoner, John Scot, was provided with an average of four pence a day for the poor in her accounts of 1265, in addition to table scraps and an occasional full dinner. Not all the nobility were as generous. Bogo de Clare, an avid collector of rich benefices, was notoriously stingy. Bogo gave a banquet in 1285 for which the food-and-drink bill was a sizeable eight pounds six shillings, with additional payments of six shillings eight pence to one wafer maker (the king's, incidentally), four shillings to another, and five shillings to a harpist. At the end of the list of the day's expenses came the item: "On the same day in alms, one penny."

Besides the official departments of the household, there were personal attendants: the ladies-in-waiting, who were not servants but companions, of slightly lower rank than the lady of the castle; the chambermaids; the barber, who also functioned as a surgeon, bloodletter, and dentist; and the doctor.

A large retinue moved with the lord from one of his castles to another. Pack horses carried household goods— one horse loaded with the lord's dismantled bed, sheets, rugs, furs, and mattress, another with the wardrobe, another with the buttery, others with kitchen furniture, candles, portable altar, and chapel furnishings. Two-wheeled carts and less maneuverable but more capacious four-wheeled wagons, built of timber with wooden wheels rimmed with iron strakes, studded with nails with projecting heads that aided traction, carried the heaviest goods, such as wine, cloth, and armor. Sometimes they carried window glass from castle to castle. Lord, lady, children, and guests rode chargers and palfreys with embroidered and gilded saddles. Matthew Paris described the traveling household of Earl Richard of Gloucester on a trip to France in 1250 as including "forty knights, equipped in new accoutrements, all alike, mounted on beautiful horses, bearing new harness, glittering with gold, and with five wagons and fifty sumpter-horses."

By the late thirteenth century, the usual horseback travel was supplemented for noble ladies by the covered chariot. Devoid of springs, the new vehicle represented little technological advance over the baggage carts. Not until the late fourteenth century did the "rocking chariot" (*chariot branlant*) appear, with strap or chain suspension. What the thirteenth-century chariot lacked in comfort it sought to make up in elegance, often being painted or gilded and covered with leather or fine wool cloth in bright colors.

If travel was uncomfortable for lords and ladies, it was rougher for the staff. When night fell on the road, the best, or only, available lodgings went to the lord's family and chief officials. Peter of Blois, a member of the household of Henry II, found that traveling even with the king was an ordeal. He and his fellow courtiers, wandering around in the dark at the place of bivouac, were fortunate if they came upon "some vile and sordid hovel," which they sometimes fought over with drawn swords.

Though most of the permanent staff, comprising the chief servants, journeyed with the lord and lady, many casual servants hired locally—grooms, huntsmen, kitchen boys, tenders of mews and kennels—were dismissed to be rehired on the lord's return. It was an opportunity to weed out bad servants, a chronic problem for every lord of a castle. Bishop Robert Grosseteste advised the countess of Lincoln to observe servants' behavior to see that porters, ushers, and marshals were courteous to guests, and to see that her liveried knights and gentlemen were carefully dressed and did not wear "old tunics, dirty cloaks and shoddy jackets." Servants should be kept on a tight leash and seldom allowed to go home for a holiday. He concluded: "No one should be kept in your household if you have not reasonable belief that he is faithful, discreet, painstaking, and honest, and of good manners."

VI

A Day in
the Castle

THE CASTLE HOUSEHOLD WAS ASTIR AT DAYBREAK. Roused
from their pallets in the attics and cellars, servants lighted
fires in kitchen and great hall. Knights and men-at-arms
clambered to the walls and towers to relieve the night
watch. In the great chamber, the lord and lady awakened
in their curtained bed.

They slept naked, and before rising put on linen under-
garments—drawers for the lord, a long chemise for the lady.
After washing in a basin of cold water, they donned outer
garments, essentially the same for both: a long-sleeved
tunic, slipped over the head and fastened at the neck with a
brooch; a second tunic, or surcoat, over it, shorter, and
either sleeveless or with wide, loose sleeves, and often
fur-lined; finally a mantle, made from an almost circular
piece of material, lined with fur and fastened at the neck
either with another brooch or with a chain. The lord's

garments were shorter than the lady's, with looser sleeves. Both wore belts tied at the waist or fastened with a metal buckle. The man's costume was completed by long hose attached to the belt that held up his drawers, while the woman's hose, shorter, were suspended from garters below the knee. Both wore shoes—slippers for the house, low boots for outdoors.

The colors of tunics, mantles, hose, and shoes were bright—blues, yellows, crimsons, purples, greens—and the fabric of the garments was usually wool, though fine silks such as samite, sendal (taffeta), and damask (a kind of brocade) were occasionally worn. Camlet, imported from Cyprus, was sometimes used for winter robes, woven from camel's or goat's hair. The fur trimmings and linings were of squirrel, lambskin, rabbit, miniver, otter, marten, beaver, fox, ermine, and sable. Tunics and mantles were decorated with embroidery, tassels, feathers, or pearls. For festive occasions belts might be of silk with gold or silver thread, or adorned with jewels. Both men and women wore head coverings indoors and outdoors. The lord usually wore a linen coif tied by strings under the chin, sometimes elaborately embroidered, or decorated with feathers and buttons; the lady wore a linen wimple, either white or colored, that covered hair and neck. Outdoors, hoods and caps were worn over the coifs and wimples. Elegant gloves, sometimes fur-lined, and jewelry—gold rings with stones, pins, necklaces, hairbands, shoebuckles, and bracelets—completed the costume.

The lady might arrange her hair with the aid of a mirror—an expensive article, usually small and circular, mounted in a wooden or metal case, and made either of polished steel or of glass over a metal surface. Despite the disapproval of preachers and moralist writers, ladies wore cosmetics—sheep fat, and rouge and skin whiteners with which they tinted themselves pink and white—and used depilatory pastes. ·

After mass in the chapel, the household breakfasted on bread washed down with wine or ale. The morning was spent in routine tasks or amusements, depending on whether the castle had guests. The lord had his round of conferences with stewards and bailiffs, or with members of his council; the lady conversed with her guests or busied herself with embroidery and other domestic projects. Knights and squires practiced fencing and tilting, while children did their lessons under the guidance of a tutor, commonly the chaplain or one of his clerks. Lessons over, the children were free to play—girls with dolls, boys with tops and balls, horseshoes, bows and arrows.

Archery was a favorite pastime with boys of all ages. In the twelfth century the son of the lord of Haverford Castle in Wales, and two other boys sent there for their education, made friends with an outlaw confined in the castle who fashioned arrows for their bows. One day the robber took advantage of the negligence of the guards to seize the boys and barricade himself in his prison. "A great clamor instantly arose," recorded the chronicler Gerald of Wales, "as well from the boys within as from the people without; nor did he cease, with an uplifted axe, to threaten the lives of the children, until indemnity and security were assured to him."

In the castle courtyard the grooms swept out the stables and fed the horses; the smith worked at his forge on horseshoes, nails, and wagon fittings; and domestic servants emptied basins and chamber pots and brought in rushes for the freshly swept floors. The laundress soaked sheets, tablecloths, and towels in a wooden trough containing a solution of wood ashes and caustic soda; then she pounded them, rinsed them, and hung them to dry. In the kitchen the cook and his staff turned the meat—pork, beef, mutton, poultry, game—on a spit and prepared stews and soups in great iron cauldrons hung over the fire on a hook and chain that could be raised and lowered to regulate the tempera-

Swinging. (Bodleian Library. MS. Bod. 264, f. 78v)

ture. Boiled meat was lifted out of the pot with an iron meat hook, a long fork with a wooden handle and prongs attached to the side. Soup was stirred with a long-handled slotted spoon.

Meat preservation was by salting or smoking, or, most commonly and simply, by keeping the meat alive till needed. Salting was done by two methods. Dry-salting meant burying the meat in a bed of salt pounded to a powder with mortar and pestle. Brine-curing consisted of immersing the meat in a strong salt solution. Before cooking, the salted meat had to be soaked and rinsed.

In addition to roasting and stewing, meat might be pounded to a paste, mixed with other ingredients, and served as a kind of custard. A dish of this kind was *blankmanger,* consisting of a paste of chicken blended with rice boiled in almond milk, seasoned with sugar, cooked until very thick, and garnished with fried almonds and anise. Another was a *mortrews,* of fish or meat that was pounded, mixed with bread crumbs, stock, and eggs, and poached, producing a kind of *quenelle,* or dumpling. Both meat and fish were also made into pies, pasties, and fritters.

A cockfight. (Bodleian Library. MS. Bod. 264, f. 50)

Sauces were made from herbs from the castle garden that were ground to a paste, mixed with wine, *verjuice* (the juice of unripe grapes), vinegar, onions, ginger, pepper, saffron, cloves, and cinnamon. Mustard, a favorite ingredient, was used by the gallon.

In Lent or on fast days fish was served fresh from the castle's own pond, from a nearby river, or from the sea, nearly always with a highly seasoned sauce. Salt or smoked herring was a staple, as were salted or dried cod and stockfish. Fresh herring, flavored with ginger, pepper, and cinnamon, might be made into a pie. Other popular fish included mullet, shad, sole, flounder, plaice, ray, mackerel, salmon, and trout. Sturgeon, whale, and porpoise were rare seafood delicacies, the first two "royal fish," fit for kings and queens. Pike, crab, crayfish, oysters, and eels were also favorites. A royal order to the sheriff of Gloucester in the 1230s stated that

> since after lampreys all fish seem insipid to both the king and the queen, the sheriff shall procure by purchase or otherwise as many lampreys as possible in his bailiwick, place them in bread and jelly, and send them to the king while he is at a

Roasting pigs on a spit, from the Luttrell Psalter. (Trustees of the British Museum. MS. Add. 42130, f. 206v)

distance from those parts by John of Sandon, the king's cook, who is being sent to him. When the king comes nearer, he shall send them to him fresh.

The most common vegetables, besides onions and garlic, were peas and beans. Staples of the diet of the poor, for the rich they might be served with onions and saffron. Honey, commonly used for sweetening, came from castle or manor bees; fruit from the castle orchard—apples, pears, plums, and peaches—was supplemented by wild fruits and nuts from the lord's wood. In addition to these local products, there were imported luxuries such as sugar (including a special kind made with roses and violets), rice, almonds, figs, dates, raisins, oranges, and pomegranates, purchased in town or at the fairs. Ordinary sugar was bought by the loaf and had to be pounded; powdered white sugar was more expensive.

At mealtimes, servants set up the trestle tables and spread the cloths, setting steel knives, silver spoons, dishes for salt, silver cups, and *mazers*—shallow silver-rimmed wooden bowls. At each place was a trencher or *manchet*, a thick slice of day-old bread serving as a plate for the roast meat. Meals were announced by a horn blown to signal time for washing hands. Servants with ewers, basins, and towels attended the guests.

At the table, seating followed status: The most important

guests were at the high table, with the loftiest place reserved for an ecclesiastical dignitary, the second for the ranking layman. After grace, the procession of servants bearing food began. First came the pantler with the bread and butter, followed by the butler and his assistants with the wine and beer. Wine, in thirteenth-century England mostly imported from English-ruled Bordeaux, was drunk young in the absence of an effective technique for stoppering containers. Wine kept a year became undrinkable. No attention was paid to vintage, and often what was served even at rich tables was of poor quality. Peter of Blois described in a letter wine served at Henry II's court: "The wine is turned sour or mouldy—thick, greasy, stale, flat and smacking of pitch. I have sometimes seen even great lords served with wine so muddy that a man must needs close his eyes and clench his teeth, wry-mouthed and shuddering, and filtering the stuff rather than drinking."

The castle bought wine by the barrel and decanted it into jugs. Some was spiced and sweetened by the butlers to go with the final course. Ale, made from barley, wheat, or oats, or all three, was drunk mainly by the servants. A castle household brewed its own, hiring an ale-wife for the task and using grain from its own stores. At the royal court, according to Peter of Blois, the ale was not much better than the wine—it was "horrid to the taste and abominable to the sight."

Ceremony marked the service at table. There was a correct way to do everything, from the laying of cloths to the cutting of trenchers and carving of meat. Part of a squire's training was learning how to serve his lord at meals: the order in which dishes should be presented, where they should be placed, how many fingers to use in holding the joint for the lord to carve, how to cut the trenchers and place them on the table.

The solid parts of soups and stews were eaten with a spoon, the broth sipped. Meat was cut up with the knife and eaten with the fingers. Two persons shared a dish, the lesser helping the more important, the younger the older, the man the woman. The former in each case broke the bread, cut the meat, and passed the cup.

Etiquette books admonished diners not to leave the spoon in the dish or put elbows on the table, not to belch, not to drink or eat with their mouths full, not to stuff their mouths or take overly large helpings. Not surprisingly, in the light of the finger-eating and dish-sharing, stress was laid on keeping hands and nails scrupulously clean, wiping spoon and knife after use, wiping the mouth before drinking, and not dipping meat in the salt dish.

The lord and lady were at pains to see their guests amply served. Bishop Robert Grosseteste advised the countess of Lincoln to make sure that her servants were judiciously distributed during dinner, that they entered the room in an orderly way and avoided quarreling. "Especially do you yourself keep watch over the service until the meats are placed in the hall, and then . . . command that your dish be so refilled and heaped up, and especially with the light dishes, that you may courteously give from your dish to all the high table on the right and on the left." At his own house, he reminded the countess, guests were served at dinner with two meats and two lighter dishes. Between courses, the steward should send the servers into the kitchen and see to it that they brought in the meats quietly and without confusion.

An everyday dinner, served between 10:00 A.M. and noon, comprised two or three courses, each of several separate dishes, all repeating the same kinds of food except the last course, which consisted of fruits, nuts, cheese, wafers, and spiced wine.

On such festive occasions as holidays and weddings, fantastic quantities of food were consumed. When Henry III's daughter married the king of Scotland on Christmas Day 1252 at York, Matthew Paris reported that "more than

Musicians. Clockwise from upper left: a psaltery, a harp, an oliphant, and a viele. (Trustees of the British Museum. MS. Ar. 157, f. 71v)

sixty pasture cattle formed the first and principal course at table . . . the gift of the archbishop. The guests feasted by turns with one king at one time, at another time with the other, who vied with one another in preparing costly meals." As for the entertainment, the number and apparel of the guests, the variety of foods: "If I were more fully to describe [them] . . . the relation would appear hyperbolical in the ears of those not present, and would give rise to ironical remarks." Such feasts included boars' heads, venison, peacocks, swans, suckling pigs, cranes, plovers, and larks.

During dinner, even on ordinary days, the party might be entertained with music or jokes and stories. Many households regularly employed harpers and minstrels. Adam the harper was a member of Bogo de Clare's household, and on occasion Bogo hired *ystriones* ("actors") and at least once a *ioculator* ("jester"), William Pilk of Salisbury. When the meal was over, one of the guests might regale the company with a song; many a knight and baron composed songs in the tradition of the trouvères, the knightly poets who were the troubadours of the North (although in some cases the tunes for their verses seem to have been written by the traveling professional minstrels known as jongleurs). They might be accompanied by the harp, the lute, or the viele, ancestor of the violin. Sometimes the accompanist played chords as a prelude to the song and as background to an occasional phrase; sometimes the singer accompanied himself in unison on the viele and played the tune over once more when he had finished singing, as a coda. The verses—in French—were sophisticated in form and stylized in subject matter, usually falling into established categories: dawn songs, spinning songs, political satires (*sirventes*), laments, debates, love songs. They might be May songs, like the following celebrated poem by Bernard de Ventadour, protégé of Eleanor of Aquitaine (the notation is modern;

medieval music was normally recorded without division into measures, the rhythm being supplied by the words—except in part-singing or polyphonic music, where more precise time was necessary for synchronization):

(When the flower appears beside the green leaf, when I see the weather bright and serene and hear in the wood the song of the birds which brings sweetness to my heart and pleases me, the more the birds sing to merit praise, the more joy I have in my heart and I must sing, as all my days are full of joy and song and I think of nothing else.)

Or they might be songs of the Crusade, like the following, by the early thirteenth-century trouvère Guiot de Dijon:

Chan-te - rai por mon co - rai-ge Que je vuil re - con-for-ter, Qu'a-vec - ques mon grant do - mai-ge Ne quier mo-rir n'a-fo - ler; Quant de la ter - re sau - va-ge Ne voi mais nul re - tor - ner, Ou cil est qui ras-so - ai-ge Mes maus quant j'en oi par - ler. *Dex, quant cri-e - rons Ou - tré-e,* *Sir, ai - diez au pe-le - rin,* *Por cui sui es-* *-po-an - té-e,* *Car fe - lon sunt Sar-ra - zin.*

(I shall sing to cheer my heart, for fear lest I die of my great grief or go mad, when I see none return from that wild land where he is who brings comfort to my heart when I hear news of him. O God, when they cry "Forward," help the pilgrim for whom I am so fearful, for the Saracens are evil.)

Or lively picaresque songs like one by Colin Muset, another thirteenth-century poet:

Quant je voi y-ver re-tor-ner Lors me vou-droi-e se-jor-ner,
Se je po-oie os-te tro-ver Lar-ge qui ne vou-sist con-ter,
Qu'e-ust porc et buef et mou-ton, Mas-larz, faisanz et ve-noi-son, Gras-
-ses ge-li-nes et cha-pons Et bons fro-ma-ges en gla-on.

(When I see winter return, then would I find lodging, if I could discover a generous host who would charge me nothing, who would have pork and beef and mutton, ducks, pheasants, and venison, fat hens and capons and good cheeses in baskets.)

Sometimes songs were sung with refrains to be repeated by a chorus; there were also lays, in which each verse had a different structure and musical setting.

The meal finished, tables were cleared, the company washed hands again, and turned to the afternoon's tasks and amusements. "The ladies and the bachelors danced and sang caroles after dinner," on a festive occasion in *The*

Left: Musician with bells. (Trustees of the British Museum. MS. Harl. 4951, f. 299v)

Right: Jester with bladder-slapstick. (Trustees of the British Museum. MS. Add. 42130, f. 167)

Castellan of Coucy. A carole was a kind of round dance in which the dancers joined hands as they sang and circled. Guests could be entertained with parlor games such as hot cockles, in which one player knelt blindfolded and was struck by the other players, whose identity he had to guess, or a variety of blind man's bluff called hoodman blind, in which a player reversed his hood to cover his face and tried to catch the others. In *The Castellan of Coucy,* "after dinner there were wine, apples, ginger; some played backgammon and chess, others went to snare falcons." Chess, widely popular, was played in two versions, one similar to the modern game, the other a simpler form played with dice. Either was commonly accompanied by gambling—the household accounts of John of Brabant on one occasion recorded two shillings lost at chess. Dice games were played in all ranks of society, and even the clergy indulged. Bogo de Clare's accounts reported three shillings handed to him on Whitsunday 1285 to play at dice. Bowls, a favorite outdoor pastime, also was accompanied by betting.

Recreation included horseplay. Matthew Paris described disapprovingly how Henry III, his half brother Geoffrey de Lusignan, and other nobles, while strolling in an orchard, were pelted with turf, stones, and green apples by one of Geoffrey's chaplains, a man "who served as a fool and buffoon to the king . . . and whose sayings, like those of a silly jester . . . excited their laughter." In the course of his buffoonery, the chaplain went so far as to press "the juice of unripe grapes in their eyes, like one devoid of sense."

Supper was served in the late afternoon. Robert Grosseteste recommended "one dish not so substantial, and also light dishes, and then cheese."

There were also late suppers, just before bedtime, drawing suspicion from such moralists as Robert Mannyng, who described midnight "rere suppers" of knights, "when their lords have gone to bed," as giving rise to gluttony and waste, not to mention lechery.

The romance *L'Escoufle* ("The Kite") pictures an evening in a castle, after supper: The count goes to relax in front of the fire in the damsels' chamber, taking off his shirt to have his back scratched and resting his head in the lap of the heroine, Aelis, while the servants stew fruits over the hearth.

The household of the castle retired early. Manuals for household management describe the activities of the chamberlain in preparing his lord for bed:

> Take off his robe and bring him a mantle to keep him from cold, then bring him to the fire and take off his shoes and his hose . . . then comb his head, then spread down his bed, lay the head sheet and the pillows, and when your

Juggler. (Trustees of the British Museum. MS. Harl. 4951, f. 298v)

The end of the day. (Trinity College, Cambridge. MS. o.9.34, f. 37r)

sovereign is in bed, draw the curtains . . . . Then drive out dog or cat, and see that there be basin and urinal set near your sovereign, then take your leave mannerly that your sovereign may take his rest merrily.

VII

Hunting as a Way of Life

AT DAWN ON A SUMMER DAY, when the deer were at their fattest, the lord, his household, and guests loved to set out into the forest. While the huntsman, a professional and often a regular member of the lord's staff, stalked the quarry with the leashed dogs and their handlers, the hunting party breakfasted in a clearing on a picnic meal of meat, wine, and bread.

When the dogs found a deer's spoor, the huntsman estimated the animal's size and age by measuring the tracks with his fingers and by studying the scratches made by the horns on bushes, the height of the rubbed-off velvet of the antlers on trees, and the "fumes" (droppings), some of which he gathered in his hunting horn to show his master. The lord made the decision as to whether it was a quarry worth hunting. Sometimes the huntsman, by silently climbing a tree, could get a sight of the deer.

The dogs were taken by a roundabout route to intercept the deer's line of retreat. They were usually of three kinds:

the lymer, a bloodhound that was kept on a leash and used to finish the stag at bay; the brachet, a smaller hound; and the greyhound or levrier, larger than the modern breed and capable of singly killing a deer.

The huntsman advanced on foot with a pair of lymers to drive the deer toward the hunting party. Meanwhile the lord raised his ivory hunting horn, the olifant, and blew a series of one-pitch notes. This was the signal for the greyhounds. Once begun, the chase continued until the hounds brought the stag to bay, when one of the hunters was given the privilege of killing it with a lance thrust. Sometimes the hunters used bows and arrows. The kill was followed by skinning and dividing up the meat, including the hounds' share, laid out on the skin.

Although the hart could be a dangerous quarry, the wild boar, usually hunted in the winter, was more formidable. A wily enemy, he would not venture out of cover without first looking, listening, and sniffing, and once his suspicions were aroused no amount of shouting and horn blowing would lure him from his narrow den. The boar-hunting dog was the alaunt, a powerful breed resembling the later German shepherd. Even when dogs and hunters caught the boar in the open, his great tusks were a fearful weapon. "I have seen them kill good knights, squires and servants," wrote Gaston de la Foix in his fourteenth-century *Livre de la Chasse* ("Book of the Hunt"). And Edward, duke of York, in the fifteenth-century treatise *The Master of Game* wrote, "The boar slayeth a man with one stroke, as with a knife. Some have seen him slit a man from knee up to breast and slay him all stark dead with one stroke." An old boar usually stood his ground and struck desperately about him, but a young boar was capable of rapid maneuvers preceding his deadly slashes.

The huntsman was always well paid, and in a great household might be a knight. Henry I employed no fewer

Hunter with longsword, accompanied by greyhound. (Trustees of the
British Museum. MS. Harl. 1585, f. 45v)

than four, at eight pence a day, at the head of a hunting company that included four horn blowers, twenty sergeants (beaters), several assistant huntsmen, a variety of dog handlers, a troop of mounted wolf hunters, and several archers, one of whom carried the king's own bow. A royal hunting party was a small military expedition.

But the form of hunting that stirred the widest interest throughout medieval Europe was falconry. Hawks were the only means of bringing down birds that flew beyond the range of arrows. Every king, noble, baron, and lord of the manor had his falcons. A favorite bird shared his master's bedroom and accompanied him daily on his wrist. Proud, fierce, and temperamental, the falcon had a mystique and a mythology. Of many treatises and manuals about falconry, the most famous was the exhaustive *De Arte Venandi cum Avibus* ("The Art of Falconry") by the erudite emperor Frederick II (from which most of the following information is drawn).

The birds used in medieval falconry belonged to two main categories. The true falcons, or long-winged hawks, included the gerfalcon, the peregrine, the saker, and the lanner, all used to hunt waterfowl, and the merlin, used for smaller birds. The short-winged hawks included the goshawk and the sparrow hawk, which could be flown in wooded country where long-winged hawks were at a disadvantage. Only the female, larger and more aggressive than the male, was properly called a falcon; the smaller male was called a tiercel, and although sometimes used in hunting was considered inferior.

One of the essential buildings in a castle courtyard was the mews where the hawks roosted and where they took refuge during molting season. It was spacious enough to allow limited flight, had at least one window, and a door large enough for the falconer to pass through with a bird on his wrist. The floor was covered with gravel or coarse sand, changed at regular intervals.

In the semidarkness inside, perches of several sizes were adapted to different kinds of birds, some high and well out from the wall, others just far enough off the floor to keep the bird's tail feathers from touching. Outside stood low wooden or stone blocks, usually in the form of cones, point down, driven into the ground with sharp iron spikes, on which the falcons "weathered," that is, became accustomed to the world outside the mews.

A good falcon was expensive chiefly because her training demanded infinite patience and care. The birds were obtained either as eyases—nestlings taken from a tree or a cliff-top—or as branchers, young birds that had just left the nest and were caught in nets. Branchers were put into a "sock," a close-fitting linen bag open at both ends, so that the bird's head protruded at one end, feet and tail at the other.

Gerald of Wales reported that once when Henry II was staying at the Clares' Pembroke Castle and "amusing himself in the country with the sport of hawking," he saw a falcon perched on a crag, and let loose on it a large

A mews. Center, a falcon is being bathed; on the right, a second falcon is being "weathered" on a block. From *De Arte Venandi cum Avibus.* (Bibliothèque Nationale. MS. Fr. 12400, f. 158)

high-bred Norway hawk. The falcon, though its flight was
at first slower than the Norway hawk's, finally rose above its
adversary, became the assailant, and pouncing on it with
great fury, laid the royal bird dead at the king's feet. "From
that time the king used to send every year in the proper
season for the young falcons which are bred in the cliffs on
the coast of South Wales; for in all his land he could not
find better or more noble hawks."

The falconer's first task was to have the bird prepared for
training. The needle points of the talons were trimmed, the
eyes usually "seeled"—temporarily sewn closed—and two
jesses, strips of leather with rings at the end, were fastened
around the legs. Small bells were tied to the feet to alert the
falconer to the bird's movements. She was then tied to the
perch by a long leather strap called a leash. At the same
time, whether seeled or not, she was usually introduced to
the hood, a piece of leather that covered her eyes, with an
opening for the beak. Now, blinded, she had to be trained
through her senses of taste, hearing, and touch.

The falcon's first lesson was learning to stand on a human
wrist. To begin with, she was carried gently about in a
darkened room for a day and a night, and passed from hand
to hand, without being fed. On the second day, the falconer
fed her a chicken leg, while talking or singing to her, always
using the same phrase or bar of a song, stroking her while
she ate. Gradually the bird was unseeled, at night or in a
darkened room, with the attendant being careful not to let
her see his face, on the theory that the human face was
particularly repugnant to the falcon. Again she was carried
about for a day and a night and fed in small quantities
while being gently stroked, and gradually she was exposed
to more light. When she was well accustomed to the new
situation, she was taken outdoors before dawn, and brought
back while it was still dark. Finally her eyesight was fully
restored, and the falconer exposed her to full daylight.

The initial stage of her training was accomplished: The captive was partially tamed and accustomed to handling. But the falconer still had to guard the sensitive, excitable creature closely to prevent her from taking alarm and injuring herself. If she became restless and tried to fly off her perch, or bit at her jesses and bell and scratched at her head, she had to be quieted by gentle speech, stroking, and feeding, or by being sprinkled with drops of water, sometimes from the falconer's mouth (which had first to be scrupulously cleansed). Once the bird felt at home on her master's wrist outdoors, she was taken on horseback.

Now the falcon was ready to be taught to return to her master during the hunt by means of the lure. This device was usually made of the wings of the bird which was to be the falcon's quarry, tied to a piece of meat. If a gerfalcon, a bird distinguished by its size, dignity, speed, and agility, was to be used to hunt cranes, the lure was made of a pair of crane's wings tied together with a leather thong, in the same position as if folded on the crane's back. To the lure was tied a long strap. To keep the falcon from flying away during these first departures from his fist, the falconer fastened a long slender cord, the creance, to the end of her leash.

In the field, as much of the line was unwound as was necessary for the bird's flight, and she was taken on the falconer's fist. An assistant handed him the lure as he removed the falcon's hood, at the same time repeating the familiar notes or words that he always used while feeding her. The falconer held firmly onto her jesses while she tasted the meat fastened to the lure. Then his assistant took the lure and moved away with it, always keeping it in the falcon's vision, finally placing it on the ground and withdrawing, while the falconer released the bird, letting the line run through his free hand. When the falcon landed on the lure, the assistant slowly approached her, holding

Falconers sprinkling their birds with water from their mouths to calm them. From *De Arte Venandi*. (Bibliothèque Nationale. MS. Fr. 12400, f. 157)

meat out, repeating her call notes, and finally setting it down before her. While she seized it, he picked her up on the lure, and gathered the jesses and drew them tight.

Once the falcon responded well to the lure, she was taught to come to it when it was whirled in the air by the assistant while he uttered the call notes. Finally the falcon sprang eagerly from the fist when she saw the lure and flew directly to it. The creance was now abandoned and the bird could be allowed to fly free.

Now she was ready to be taught to hunt. A gerfalcon to be used in hunting cranes was often started on hares, because the same method of flight was used for both, and because a hare would be unlikely to distract a falcon when she hunted for cranes, since hares always had to be driven out of cover by dogs. Sometimes a stuffed rabbit pelt baited with meat was dragged in front of the falcon, with the falconer on horseback racing over the fields after the decoy, letting the falcon loose only to jerk her up short before she could strike, teaching her to swoop and pounce suddenly.

Then the falconer brought out the hounds, who drove live rabbits out for the falcon.

Next the gerfalcon was exposed to snipe and partridge. Only when she became proficient with these was she ready for her real quarry, and even now her introduction was gradual. At first a live crane was staked in a meadow, its eyes seeled, its claws blunted, and its beak bound so that it could not injure the gerfalcon. Meat was tied to its back. The gerfalcon was unhooded and the crane shown to her. When the falcon killed the crane, the falconer removed its heart and fed it to the falcon. The process was repeated, increasing the distance between the mounted falconer and the crane bait until the gerfalcon began her flight a bowshot away (300 to 400 yards). At the same time the falconer trained the falcon to recognize a crane's call by slitting a crane's larynx and blowing into it.

Dogs, usually greyhounds, were often used in teaching the gerfalcon to capture larger birds. This meant special training for the dogs as well as the falcons, so that the dog did not desert the hunt to chase a rabbit. Dog and falcon were fed together to enhance their comradeship, while the dog was trained to run with the falcon and help her seize her prey.

A different technique was used for "hawking at the brook," that is, hunting ducks on the riverbank. Here the hawk was trained to circle above the falconer's head, "waiting on," while the hounds raised the ducks. She then "stooped" (dived) to strike them in the air.

The good falconer, according to Frederick II, who employed more than fifty in his Apulian castles, had to be of medium size—not too large to be agile and not too small to be strong. Besides the cardinal virtue of patience, the falconer needed acute hearing and vision, a daring spirit, alert mind, and even temper. He could not be a heavy sleeper, lest he fail to hear the falcon's bells in the night. And he had to be well versed in the ailments of hawks and

Falconers carrying hawks. From *De Arte Venandi*. (Bibliothèque Nationale. MS. Fr. 12400, f. 155v)

their remedies—medicines for headaches and colds, salves for injuries: mixtures of spices, vinegar, snakemeat, gristle, and drugs almost as unpleasant as the medicines prescribed for human beings.

Hunting was much more than a sport, and the forest much more than a recreation ground. The deer and other quarry supplied a substantial share of the meat for the castle table, and the forest supplemented game with nuts, berries, mushrooms, and other wild edibles. It also furnished the principal construction material and fuel for all classes. King Henry III granted ten oaks from the Forest of Dean in 1228 to William Marshal II to use in remodeling and heightening Fitz Osbern's Great Tower; later he granted more oaks to Gilbert Marshal to finish the work. Forest land was a natural resource of immense value, and consequently coveted, defended, and fought over. William the Conqueror, a great lover of hunting, brought "forest law" from France to England to preserve the English forests for his own use. Medieval land clearance and sheep grazing had had a major impact on the ecology of Europe (something like that of agricultural expansion on North America in the nineteenth century), and although William and other European princes who enacted regulations were not interested in ecology, their actions had the effect of curbing deforestation.

Stringent prohibitions were promulgated against poaching. *The Anglo-Saxon Chronicle* reported:

> William set aside a vast deer preserve and imposed laws concerning it, so that whoever slew a hart or hind was to be blinded. He forbade the killing of boars, even as the killing of harts, for he loved the tall deer as if he had been their father . . . . The rich complained, and the poor lamented, but he was so stern that he cared not though all might hate him.

William established as royal forest or game preserve large tracts that embraced villages and wasteland as well as woods. On these lands no one but the king and those authorized by him—not even the barons who held the land—could hunt the red deer, the fallow deer, the roe, and the wild boar. Hounds and bows were forbidden. Because foxes, hares, badgers, squirrels, wild cats, martens, and otter were considered harmful to the deer and boar, rights of "warren" were often granted for hunting these smaller quarry. Birds hunted in falconry were generally also included in the "beasts of the warren," although they were not harmful to the deer. Dogs kept within the forest had to be "lawed"—three talons cut from each front foot.

The twelfth-century chronicler Florence of Worcester attributed the death of the Conqueror's son, William Rufus, in a hunting accident in the New Forest (south of Winchester), to his father's strict forest laws.

> Nor can it be wondered that . . . Almighty power and vengeance should have been thus displayed. For in former times . . . this tract of land was thickly planted with churches and with inhabitants who were worshippers of God; but by command of King William the elder the people were

expelled, the houses half ruined, the churches pulled down, and the land made an habitation for wild beasts only; and hence, as it is believed, arose this mischance. For Richard, the brother of William the younger, had perished long before in the same forest, and a short time previously his cousin Richard, the [natural] son of Robert, earl [duke] of Normandy, was also killed by an arrow by one of his knights, while he was hunting. A church, built in the old times, had stood on the spot where the king fell, but as we have already said, it was destroyed in the time of his father.

William Rufus' death was vividly pictured by Ordericus Vitalis:

[That morning—August 1, 1100] King William, having dined with his minions, prepared, after the meal was ended, to go forth and hunt in the New Forest. Being in great spirits, he was joking with his attendants while his boots were being laced, when an armorer came and presented to him six arrows. The king immediately took them with great satisfaction, praising the work, and unconscious of what was to happen, kept four of them himself and gave the other two to Walter Tirel [lord of Poix and castellan of Pontoise, fifteen miles northwest of Paris]. "It is but right," he said, "that the sharpest arrows should be given to him who knows best how to inflict mortal wounds with them." . . . [The king] hastily rose, and mounting his horse, rode at full speed to the forest. His brother, Count Henry, with William de Breteuil [son of William Fitz Osbern] and other distinguished persons followed him, and, having penetrated into the woods, the hunters dispersed themselves in various directions according to custom. The king and Walter posted themselves with a few others in one part of the forest, and stood with their weapons in their hands eagerly watching for the coming of the game, when a stag suddenly running between them, the king quitted his station, and Walter shot an arrow. It grazed the beast's horny back, but glancing from it, mortally wounded the king who stood within its range. He immediately fell to the ground, and alas! suddenly expired . . . . Some of the servants wrapped the king's bloody corpse in a mean covering, and brought it, like a wild boar pierced by the hunters, to the city of Winchester.

Henry II, William Rufus' great-nephew, was another enthusiastic hunter. According to Gerald of Wales,

> He was immoderately fond of the chase, and devoted himself to it with excessive ardor. At the first dawn of day he would mount a fleet horse, and indefatigably spend the day in riding through the woods, penetrating the depths of forests, and crossing the ridges of hills . . . . He was inordinately fond of hawking or hunting, whether his falcons stooped on their prey, or his sagacious hounds, quick of scent and swift of foot, pursued the chase. Would to God he had been as zealous in his devotions as he was in his sports!

By the thirteenth century, forest law was even more strictly enforced in England than on the Continent, where there were fewer royal forests and more grants of hunting rights. William I's successors had persistently striven to extend the area of the royal forest, although Richard I and John, when they needed money, "disafforested" large areas, opening them to local lords in return for cash payments. In 1217, under William Marshal's regency in the early years of Henry III's reign, the Forest Charter was granted as a kind of postscript to Magna Carta, to further satisfy the barons. By it the forest law was codified and a commission directed to make "perambulations" of the royal forest, reviewing additions made under Henry II, Richard, and John, and retaining only those that were in the king's own demesne. Ten years later, when Henry came of age, he summoned the knights who had made the perambulations and forced them to revise their boundaries in the royal favor. The forest then remained essentially unchanged until 1300, when Edward I was forced once more to disafforest large tracts.

The Forest Charter designated the courts to enforce forest law: local courts that met regularly every six weeks, special forest inquisitions called to deal with serious trespasses, and the royal forest eyre (circuit court) that had ultimate jurisdiction. The local attachment courts dealt with minor offenses to the "vert"—the greenwood of the forest: cutting; clearing; gathering dead wood, honey, and nuts; allowing cattle to graze or pigs to feed on acorns and beechnuts. When a graver offense against the vert or a crime against the "venison"—the right to hunt deer—was committed, a special court was called to hear the case before the forest officers, and either send the offender to prison until the next eyre or attach him to appear before it, depending on the seriousness of the crime. Any evidence—arrows, antlers, skins, poachers' greyhounds—was delivered to forest officials to be produced before the justices (the deer was usually given to the poor, the sick, or lepers). Sentence to imprisonment by the special inquisition was not punishment, but merely insurance that the accused would duly appear before the eyre. If the accused could find pledges to secure his appearance, he was released.

Every seven years the forest eyre, made up of four barons and knights appointed by the king, traveled from county to county hearing the accumulated forest cases. Trespassers were brought from prison or produced by the sheriff; the foresters and other officers presented their exhibits and the record of the special inquisition. The record was usually accepted as proof of the facts without any further hearing of evidence, and the prisoner was sentenced to prison for a year and a day—again not as punishment but against the payment of a ransom or fine. Usually the fine was in proportion to the prisoner's condition, and sometimes trespassers were pardoned because they were poor. If a man had spent much time in jail waiting to be tried, he was released: "And because Roger lay for a long time in prison, so that he is nearly dead, it is judged that he go quit; and let him dwell outside the forest." "Because he was a long time in prison and has no goods, therefore he is quit thereof." On the other hand, if he failed to appear, the trespasser was outlawed.

Every three years an inspection of the forests was made by a body of twelve knights, the "regarders," who were supposed to report any encroachments on the king's demesne—the erection of a mill or a fishpond, the enlargement of a clearing, the enclosure of land without license, or any abuse of the right to cut wood.

Besides the regarders, the forest was administered by a large hierarchy of officials, headed by the justice, who directed the whole forest administration of England. Next in authority were the wardens, also called stewards, bailiffs, or chief foresters, who had custody of single forests or groups of forests; below them were officers called verderers, knights or landed gentry nominally in charge of the vert but actually with a variety of duties; and there were also foresters, who acted as gamekeepers, responsible to the wardens and appointed by them. Usually each forest had four agisters, too, appointed by the wardens to collect money for the pasturing of cattle and pigs in the king's demesne woods and lawns, allowed at certain seasons. The agisters counted the pigs as they entered the forest and collected the pennies as they came out. Landowners inside the forest also employed woodwards, their own foresters.

On their estates many barons set up private forests or "chases," either on wooded country not under forest law or by receiving from the king grants of "vert and venison." By the reign of Edward I, the royal forest of Dean, in Gloucestershire, north and east of Chepstow, contained the private chases of thirty-six landowners, mostly the great magnates of the region, including the lord of Chepstow, Earl Roger Bigod; the abbot of St. Peter's, Gloucester; the bishop of Hereford; the earl of Lancaster; the earl of Warwick; and Baron Richard Talbot.

Once the king had granted a forest to a subject, royal forest law was suspended and royal forest justices and courts surrendered jurisdiction to the baron who owned the chase. The baron's foresters could arrest trespassers against the venison, but only when they were caught "with the mainour," in the act and with the evidence. Then they were held in prison until they paid a fine to the lord.

Sometimes districts were enclosed with palings or ditches and became parks. Later such enclosures had to be licensed by the king, but in the time of Henry III a license was not necessary as long as there was no infringement on the royal forest. The baron who created a park, however, was obliged to keep it effectively enclosed so that the king's beasts did not enter it. Some owners of parks neighboring the royal forests evaded the law by building sunken fences called deer leaps so designed that the king's deer could leap them to enter the park, but once in could not get out again. Forest courts often ordered deer leaps removed, and even ruled certain parks close to the forest legal "nuisances" because the owner might be moved to entice the king's deer into the enclosure.

Ecclesiastical as well as lay landlords established their own preserves. In the twelfth century Abbot Samson of Bury St. Edmunds, according to Jocelin of Brakelond, "enclosed many parks, which he replenished with beasts of chase, keeping a huntsman with dogs; and upon the visit of any person of quality, sat with his monks in some walk of the wood, and sometimes saw the coursing of the dogs; but I never saw him take part in the sport." Other prelates joined in the hunt.

An exception to forest law was provided for the earl or baron traveling through a royal forest. Either in the presence of a forester, or while blowing his hunting horn to show that he was not a poacher, he was allowed to take a deer or two for the use of his party. The act was carefully recorded in the rolls of the special forest inquisitions under the title "Venison taken without warrant." A roll of Northamptonshire of 1248 read:

> The lord bishop of Lincoln took a hind and a roe in Bulax on the Tuesday next before Christmas Day in the thirtieth year

[of the reign of Henry III]. Sir Guy de Rochefort took a doe and a doe's brocket [a hind of the second year] in the park of Brigstock in the vigil of the Purification of the Blessed Mary in the same year . . . .

Deer killed with the king's permission were listed as "venison given by the lord king":

The countess of Leicester had seven bucks in the forest of Rockingham of the gift of the lord king on the feast of the apostles Peter and Paul . . . . Aymar de Lusignan had ten bucks in the same forest . . . . Sir Richard, earl of Cornwall, came into the forest of Rockingham about the time of the feast of the Assumption of the Blessed Mary, and took beasts in the park and outside the park at his pleasure in the thirty-second year . . . . Sir Simon de Montfort had twelve bucks in the bailiwick of Rockingham of the gift of the lord king about the time of the feast of St. Peter's Chains in the thirty-second year.

The records of the forest courts were full of dramatic episodes.

A certain hart entered the bailiwick of the castle of Bridge by the postern; and the castellans of Bridge took it and carried it to the castle. And the verderers on hearing this came there and demanded of Thomas of Ardington, who was then the sheriff, what he had done with the hart . . . . The township of Bridge was attached for the same hart.

Sir Hugh of Goldingham, the steward of the forest, and Roger of Tingewick, the riding forester, . . . perceived a man on horseback and a page following him with a bow and arrows, who forthwith fled. Wherefore he was hailed on account of his flight by the said Hugh and Roger; and he was followed . . . and taken, as he fled, outside the covert, with his surcoat bloody and turned inside out. He was asked whence that blood came, and he confessed that it came from a certain roe, which he had killed . . . .

> When Maurice de Meht, who said that he was with Sir Robert Passelewe, passed in the morning with two horses through the town of Sudborough, he saw three men carrying a sack . . . . And when the aforesaid three men saw him following them, they threw away the sack and fled. And the said Maurice de Meht took the sack and found in it a doe, which had been flayed, and a snare, with which the beast had been taken . . . .

Clerical as well as lay hunters became embroiled with the law or with their neighbors. In 1236 at the coronation of Queen Eleanor, the earl of Arundel was unable to take part in the ceremony because he had been excommunicated by the archbishop of Canterbury for seizing the archbishop's hounds when the archbishop hunted in the earl's forest.

In 1254 a poacher, in the employ of the parson of Easton, was imprisoned for taking a "beast" in the hedge of Rockingham Castle. Freed from prison on pledge, the poacher died, but the parson, Robert Bacon, who had apparently also taken part in the hunt, and Gilbert, the doorkeeper of the castle, were ordered to appear. At the hearing Sir John Lovet, a forest official who may have been bribed by the accused, declared that the "beast" was not a deer but a sheep. The accused men were acquitted, but John Lovet was imprisoned for contradicting his own records, and released only after the payment of a fine of twelve marks.

One night in 1250 foresters found a trap in Rockingham Forest and nearby heard a man cutting wood. Lying in wait, they surprised Robert Le Noble, chaplain of Sudborough, with a branch of green oak and an axe. The next morning they searched his house and found arrows and a trap that bore traces of the hair of a deer. The chaplain was arrested at once and his chattels, wheat, oats, beans, wood, dishes, and a mare were seized as pledges for his appearance before the forest eyre. Another cleric was one of a company that spent a day in 1272 shooting in the forest, killing eight deer. Cutting off the head of a buck, they stuck it on the end of a pole in a clearing and put a spindle in its mouth, and in the words of the court rolls, "they made the mouth gape towards the sun, in great contempt of the lord king and his foresters."

Sometimes malefactors used clerical privilege to obtain release from prison, as when in 1255 one Gervais of Dene, servant of John of Crakehall, archdeacon of Bedford and later the king's treasurer, was arrested for poaching and lodged in the prison of Huntingdon. The vicar of Huntingdon, several chaplains, and a servant of the bishop of Lincoln came to the prison armed with book and candle, claiming that Gervais was a clerk and threatening to excommunicate the foresters. Taking off the prisoner's cap, they exposed a shaven head. Gervais was allowed to escape, though the foresters suspected that he had been shaved that day in prison. But at the forest eyre of Huntingdon in 1255 John of Crakehall was fined ten marks for harboring Gervais, who along with the vicar was turned over to the archdeacon of Huntingdon to deal with.

Usually the sons of knights or freeholders, foresters often abused their powers for gain—felling trees, grazing their own cattle, embezzling, taking bribes, extorting "sheaves, cats, corn, lambs and little pigs" from the people at harvest time (although specifically forbidden to do so by the Forest Charter), and killing the very deer they were supposed to protect. Not only the people who lived within the royal forests, but the nobles suffered. Matthew Paris complained that a knight named Geoffrey Langley, marshal of the king's household, made an inquisition into the royal forests in 1250 and

> forcibly extorted such an immense sum of money, especially from nobles of the northern parts of England, that the amount collected exceeded the belief of all who heard of it . . . . The aforesaid Geoffrey was attended by a large and well-armed retinue, and if any one of the aforesaid nobles

made excuses . . . he ordered him to be at once taken and consigned to the king's prison . . . . For a single small beast, a fawn, or hare, although straying in an out-of-the-way place, he impoverished men of noble birth, even to ruin, sparing neither blood nor fortune.

Villagers in forest areas were supposed to raise the "hue and cry" (shouting when a felony was committed and turning out with weapons to pursue the malefactor) when an offense had been committed against the forest law. But their sympathies were often with the poachers. Again and again the rolls of the forest courts record the statements of the neighboring villages that they "knew nothing," "recognized nobody," "suspected no one," "knew of no malefactor."

Forest officers were a hated class. A Northamptonshire inquisition of 1251 recorded an exchange between a verderer and an acquaintance he met in the forest who refused to greet him, declaring, "Richard, I would rather go to my plow than serve in such an office as yours."

Many of the accounts of the forest inquests have the ring of Robin Hood, whose legend, significantly, sprang up in the thirteenth century. In May 1246 foresters in Rockingham Forest heard that there were poachers "in the lawn of Beanfield with greyhounds for the purpose of doing evil to the venison of the lord king." After waiting in ambush, they

saw five greyhounds, of which one was white, another black, the third fallow, a fourth black spotted, hunting beasts, which greyhounds the said William and Roger [the foresters] seized. But the fifth greyhound, which was tawny, escaped. And when the aforesaid William and Roger returned to the forest after taking the greyhounds, they lay in ambush and saw five poachers in the lord king's demesne of Wydehawe, one with a crossbow and four with bows and arrows, standing at their trees. And when the foresters perceived them, they hailed and pursued them.

And the aforesaid malefactors, standing at their trees,

turned in defense and shot arrows at the foresters so that they wounded Matthew, the forester of the park of Brigstock, with two Welsh arrows, to wit with one arrow under the left breast, to the depth of one hand slantwise, and with the second arrow in the left arm to the depth of two fingers, so that it was despaired of the life of the said Matthew. And the foresters pursued the aforesaid malefactors so vigorously that they turned and fled into the thickness of the wood. And the foresters on account of the darkness of the night could follow them no more. And thereupon an inquisition was made at Beanfield before William of Northampton, then bailiff [warden] of the forest, and the foresters of the country . . . by four townships neighboring . . . to wit, by Stoke, Carlton, Great Oakley, and Corby.

Stoke comes and being sworn says that it knows nothing thereof except only that the foresters attacked the malefactors with hue and cry until the darkness of night came, and that one of the foresters was wounded. And it does not know whose were the greyhounds.

Carlton comes, and being sworn, says the same.

Corby comes, and being sworn, says the same.

Great Oakley comes, and being sworn, says that it saw four men and one tawny greyhound following them, to wit one with a crossbow and three with bows and arrows, and it hailed them and followed them with the foresters until the darkness of night came, so that on account of the darkness of night and the thickness of the wood it knew not what became of them . . . .

The arrows with which Matthew was wounded, were delivered to Sir Robert Basset and John Lovet, verderers.

The greyhounds were sent to Sir Robert Passelewe, then justice of the forest.

Matthew died of his wounds, and a later inquisition revealed that Matthew's brother and two other foresters had seen the same three greyhounds in April when dining with the abbot of Pipewell, and that they belonged to one Simon of Kivelsworthy, who was thereupon sent to Northampton to be imprisoned. The abbot of Pipewell had to answer before the justices for harboring Simon and his greyhounds. The case was later brought before the forest eyre in Northampton in 1255, where Simon proved that his greyhounds "were led there by him at another time but not then," and was released after paying a fine of half a mark. The real culprit was never found.

VIII

The Villagers

Quoth Piers Plowman, "By Saint Peter of Rome!
I have an half acre to plow by the highway;
Once I have plowed this half acre and sown it after,
I will wend with you and show you the way . . .
I shall give them food if the land does not fail,
Meat and bread both to rich and to poor, as long as I live,
For the love of heaven; and all manner of men
That live through meat and drink, help him to work wightly
Who wins your food . . ."

And would that . . . Piers with his plows . . .
Were emperor of all the world, and then perhaps all men would be Christian!

Though many castles were built inside towns for political
and strategic reasons, the castle was rooted economically in
the countryside. It was connected intimately with the
village and the manor, the social and economic units of
rural Europe. The village was a community, a collective

settlement, with its own ties, rights, and obligations. The manor was an estate held by a lord and farmed by tenants who owed him rents and services, and whose relations with him were governed by his manorial court. A manor might coincide with a village, or it might contain more than one village, or a village might contain parts of manors or several entire manors.

The manor supplied the castle's livelihood. The word "manor" came to England with the Conqueror, but the arrangement was centuries old. On the Continent, it was used to provide a living for the knight and his retainers at a time when money was scarce.

A great castle such as Chepstow commanded a large number of manors, often widely scattered and interspersed with land belonging to other lords. The kind of settlement and cultivation on these manors depended on their location. On most of the plain of northern Europe, and in England in a band running southwest from the North Sea through the Midlands to the English Channel, the land lay in great open stretches of field broken here and there by stands of trees and the clustered houses of villages. This was "champion" ("champagne," open field) country. Contrasting with it was the "woodland" country of Brittany and Normandy and the west, northwest, and southeast of England, where small, compact fields were marked off with hedges and ditches, and the farmhouses were scattered in tiny hamlets.

In champion country, the villages were large, with populations of several hundred. The surrounding fields were divided into either two or three sectors, farmed according to a traditional rotation of crops. In each sector every villager held strips of land, alongside and mixed in with those of his fellows and those of the lord. Land usually descended to the eldest son, but younger brothers and sisters could stay on and work for the heir, as long as they remained unmarried. Many younger sons of champion country left home to seek their fortunes in the cities, or became mercenary soldiers.

In woodland country, on the other hand, each man worked his own separate farm. Land passed to all the surviving sons, who held and worked it together, living in a single large house or in a small group of adjoining houses. Tenants combined to perform labor service for their lord, but the system of inheritance made responsibility for services harder to assign. In consequence, woodland farmers tended to pay money rents instead of performing services, while in champion country the feudal work obligation tended to be the rule.

The village of champion country was typically a straggle of houses and farm buildings that had grown up along an existing road, but sometimes simply developed by itself, the paths between buildings and fields and adjacent villages over the centuries becoming worn and sunken to form the village streets. If there was a manor house, this large building, a lesser form of the castle hall, dominated the scene, along with the parish church, which on varying occasions served as storehouse, courthouse, prison, and fort. For the men in the fields, its bell sounded the alarm as well as the celebration of the mass. In its yard the villagers gathered to gossip, dance, and play games, and to hold fairs and markets.

Except in areas where stone was plentiful, houses were built of wattle and daub, that is, of timber framework supporting oak or willow wands covered with a mixture of clay, chopped straw or cow-hair, and cow-dung. In England the timber was most commonly oak. Sometimes a trunk and main branch of a tree were first trimmed of branches, then felled, split, and reassembled to form an arched "cruck" truss supporting roof and walls, strengthened with beams. The roofs were thatched. Houses were easily built, and could easily be moved—or destroyed; thieves were known to dig through house walls. The smallest huts consisted of a single room, and even in the largest, most of the household ate and slept together in the main room, still another version of the hall, with an open hearth in the middle and a smoke vent in the roof. The floor, usually of beaten earth, was covered with rushes. Sometimes there was a separate room for the owner, sometimes even one for the old grandparents, or part of the family might sleep in a loft reached by ladder and trapdoor. Typically the cattle were housed at one end of the building, under the same roof. The kitchen was often in a separate building, or in a lean-to.

A peasant's possessions consisted of three or four benches and stools, a trestle table, a chest, one or two iron or brass pots, a little pottery ware, wooden bowls, cups, and spoons, linen towels, wool blankets, iron tools, and, most important, his livestock. A reasonably prosperous villager owned hens and geese, a few skinny half-wild razor-backed hogs, a cow or even two, perhaps a couple of sheep, and his pair of plow oxen.

Outside the house, chickens scratched in the little farmyard (toft or messuage) containing one or two outbuildings, in the rear of which lay a garden plot, or croft, that the householder could farm as he pleased.

Contrary to widespread impression, the villagers of the thirteenth century were not limited to subsistence farming. They grew crops for their own households, for their payments to the lord, and sometimes for cash sales to markets. In England wheat was usually a cash crop, to be sold to pay for the money rents and taxes of the peasant household, while barley, oats, and rye were grown mainly for home consumption. Not all grains were baked into bread; some were brewed into ale. Peas and beans were usually boiled into soup. Other vegetables grew in the garden patches of the tofts and crofts—onions, cabbages, leeks. Staple crops were sown twice a year: wheat and rye in the fall, and barley, vetches, oats, peas, and beans in early

Letentur celi et exultet terra : com
moueatur mare et plenitudo eius.
Gaudebunt campi + omnia que in
is sunt

Reaping, from the Luttrell Psalter. (Trustees of the British Museum. MS. Add. 42130, f. 172v)

spring. Crops matured and were harvested in August and September.

Agricultural technology, if limited and unimaginative by the standards of a later age, was not entirely static despite the lack of scientific knowledge. The thirteenth-century farmer employed three ways to restore and improve the soil: by fallowing, that is, letting a field rest for a year; by marling, spreading a clay containing carbonate of lime; or by using sheep or cattle manure. But marl was scarce, and shortage of feed limited the number of animals and the supply of manure. To feed his cattle, the farmer had only the grass that grew in the commonly-held "water meadows," wetlands left untilled, and the stubble of the harvested fields. The advantages of planting grasses or turnips specifically for cattle feed were not yet perceived. The result was that there was never enough feed to see the livestock through the winter, and some had to be slaughtered every fall, in turn limiting the supply of manure for spring fertilizing. The technique of growing crops of clover and alfalfa to be plowed into the soil as fertilizer also was unknown.

For fallowing, the chief means of restoring the fields' fertility, the villagers used crop rotation in either the ancient two-field or the newer three-field system. In the latter, one field was plowed in the fall and sown with wheat and rye. Each villager planted his own strip of land, all with the same seed. In the spring a second field was plowed and sown to oats, peas, beans, barley, and vetches. A third field was left fallow from harvest to harvest. The next year the field that had been planted with wheat and rye was planted with the oats, barley, and legumes; the fallow field was planted with wheat and rye; and the field that had grown the spring seed was left fallow.

In the older but still widely used two-field system, one field was left fallow and the other tilled half with winter wheat and rye, half with spring seed. The next year the tilled field lay fallow and the fallow field was tilled, with winter and spring crops alternating in the sections that were planted.

The plowman was the common man of the Middle Ages, Piers Plowman, guiding his heavy iron-shod plow, sometimes mounted on wheels to make it go more evenly, cutting the ground with its coulter, breaking it with its share, and turning it over with its wooden mould-board. The medieval husbandman plowed in long narrow strips of "ridge and furrow," starting just to one side of the center line of his piece of land, plowing the length of the strip, turning at the end and plowing back along the other side, and continuing around. In the wet soil of northern Europe, this ridge-and-furrow plowing helped free the soil from standing water that threatened to drown the grain. Peas and beans were planted in the furrow, grain on the ridge. The ancient pattern of ridge and furrow can still be seen in England in fields long abandoned to grazing.

The husbandman's plow was drawn by a team of oxen whose number has provided a tantalizing mystery for scholars. Manorial records in profusion refer to teams of eight oxen, but pictorial representations nearly always show a more credible two, or occasionally four. Two men operated the plow, the plowman proper grasping the plow handles, or stilts, while his partner drove the oxen, walking to their left and shouting commands as he used a whip or goad. Behind followed men and women who broke up the clods with plow-bats or, in planting time, did the sowing.

On occasion villages increased their area under cultivation either by sowing part of the field that would normally have lain fallow or by making *assarts,* bringing wasteland under the plow. Such important measures were executed only with the agreement of all the villagers, and the land thus gained was shared equally.

Equality, in fact, was the guiding principle in the village, within the limits of two basic social classes: the more prosperous peasants, whose land was sufficient to support their families, and the cottars, who had to hire out as day-laborers to their better-off neighbors. The better-off villagers commonly held a "yardland" or a "half-yardland" (thirty or fifteen acres, or, in the terminology of northern England, two *oxgangs* or one *oxgang*). Along with these holdings went a portion of the village meadow, about two acres, the location decided by an annual lottery. At the lower end of the scale, the cottars held five acres of land or less; they had to borrow oxen from their neighbors for plowing, or were even forced to "delve," that is, cultivate with a spade. At least half an average village's holdings were in the cottar class, too small to feed a family and requiring the supplement of income gained by hiring out. In some demesnes the lord's land was cultivated chiefly or even entirely by such hired labor.

A second distinction among the villagers was based on personal rather than economic status: They were either free or non-free. Most of the villagers, whether half-yardlanders or cottars, were non-free, or villeins (the term "serf" was less common in England), which meant mainly that they owed heavy labor service to their lords: "week's work," consisting of two or three days a week throughout the year. A villein had other disabilities—he was not protected by the royal courts, but was subject to the will of his lord in the manorial courts; he could not leave his land or sell his livestock without permission; when his daughter married, he had to pay a fee; when he succeeded to his father's holding, he paid a "relief," or fine, and also a *heriot,* usually the best beast of the deceased. Most important, however, in an age of limited technology, when every hour's work was precious, was the compulsion to work on the lord's lands, plowing, mowing hay, reaping, shocking and transporting grain, threshing and winnowing, washing and shearing the lord's sheep. By the thirteenth century labor services were often commuted into money payments. But in cash or kind, approximately half of all the villein's efforts ultimately went, in one way or another, to the lord's profit.

The rents and services of a villein were described in the manor custom books, often in elaborate detail: how much land the tenant was to plow with how many oxen, whether he was to use his own horse and harrow, or fetch the seed himself from the lord's granary. Usually there were special rents for special rights—a hen at Christmas (the "wood-hen") in return for dead timber from the lord's wood, or the right to pasture cattle on some of the lord's land in return for a plowing. At certain times of crisis during the year the lord could call on all of his tenants—free and unfree—to leave their own farming and work for him, plowing, mowing, or reaping. These movable works, called *boons* or *benes,* were the longest preserved of all work services. In return, the lord gave food, drink, or money, or sometimes all three. Benes were classified accordingly—the *alebidreap* and the *waterbidreap,* when the lord gave ale or water; the *hungerbidreap,* when the villagers were obliged to bring their own food; the *dryreap,* when there was no ale. The food donated by the lord was generally plentiful—meat or fish, pea or bean soup, bread and cheese. In theory these benes were done for the lord out of love—they were "love-boons" —as for any neighbor that needed help, like the community effort of a barn-raising or a town bee. Like these, they were the occasion of social gatherings. A characteristic feature was the "sporting chance"; at the end of the working day the lord gave each hay-maker a bundle of hay as large as he could lift with his scythe, or a sheep was loosed in the field, and if the mowers could catch it they could roast it.

In every village were found at least a few free tenants. Some simply held their land free of most labor services, owing money rents and "suit," meaning attendance at certain courts. Others were the skilled craftsmen: the miller, the smith, the carpenter, the weaver, the tanner, the shoemaker. Most prosperous among these, and least popu-lar, was the miller, who paid the lord for the right to operate the mill, a strictly enforced monopoly. The villagers brought their grain there, contributing in payment the *multure,* a sixteenth to a twenty-fourth part of the grain. Since the millers did the measuring, they naturally fell under suspicion of cheating on weight. They were also accused of substituting bad grain for good. A medieval riddle asked, "What is the boldest thing in the world?" and replied, "A miller's shirt, for it clasps a thief by the throat daily." A few villagers secretly ground their grain with a hand-mill at home, but ran the risk of seizure and punishment.

The smith had the privileges of using charcoal from the lord's wood and having his land plowed by the lord's plows, in return for which he shod the lord's horses and ground his scythes and sheep shears, along with those of the villagers. The carpenter, with similar privileges, repaired the plows, carts, and harrows, and built and mended houses and furniture.

The poorest people in the village, the cottars, were sometimes free too, although they might hold nothing more than their cottages and the yards that surrounded them. When they were unfree, they owed lesser services than the more substantial villeins—"hand work" rather than plowing: spreading dung, repairing walls and thatches, digging ditches.

Given the choice between freedom and more land, any villager would have chosen land. Land, in fact, was the real freedom.

Over the majority of villagers, the landholding villeins, the lord in theory had arbitrary power. He could increase a villein's rents and services at will, or seize his holdings. In practice, however, the lord's legal position was modified by an accumulation of traditions that had the force of law. Custom was reinforced by the fact that the lord could not survive without the services of his tenants. The lord rarely pressed them so hard that they ran away, or even resisted him. Unless a tenant failed to perform his services, he remained in possession of his holding and could pass it on to his heir. Even the wood and wasteland, theoretically owned by the lord, could only be exploited within limits imposed by custom.

Lord and tenant rarely met face to face, the manor's affairs being left to the steward or bailiff. Nevertheless, the tenant-lord relationship was as reciprocal as it was real. Furthermore, it was permanent. Villeins were bound to the land, but at the same time custom ruled that they could not be deprived of their holdings. A villein could leave the manor if he paid a fine and a yearly fee while he stayed away, but leaving meant losing his land.

The village community met at intervals in an assembly called a bylaw, a term that applied to the body as well as to the rules it passed. At these bylaws, all matters were decided that were not automatically regulated by custom—the choice of herdsmen, problems of pasture and harvest, the repair of fences, and the clearing of ditches. It was decided who should be hired to glean and reap, when and how the harvesting should take place, in what order animals should be allowed to graze after the harvest. Every villager had a voice. Decisions were made not by vote but by consensus: Everyone expressed his view, but once a general agreement emerged from the discussion, it became unanimous. No lengthy disagreement was tolerated, and the stubborn or rebellious were threatened with fines.

The bylaws of an Oxfordshire manor in 1293 declared: "No one shall in time of autumn receive anyone as a gleaner who is able to do the work of a reaper." In other words, able-bodied men, strong enough to swing a scythe in reaping, were not to do gleaning—gathering the grain after the reapers were finished—a job reserved for elders and women. Second, "No one shall give anyone sheaves in the field." Reapers who received their wages in sheaves were not to carry them off from the fields; to prevent stealing, the sheaves had to be taken to the villagers' own homes and given out by the man from whose lands they came. Third, "No one shall enter the fields with a cart to carry grain after sunset; . . . none shall enter the fields except at the village entrances; . . . all grain . . . gathered in the fields shall be borne out openly through the midst of the town and not secretly by back ways." In this way the villagers could watch everyone who came and went during the harvest.

A bylaw of 1329 read: "No one shall take in outsiders or

natives who behave themselves badly in the gleaning or
elsewhere . . . . Also, no one may tether horses in the fields
amid growing grain or grain that has been reaped where
damage can arise. Also, no one may make paths, by
walking or driving or carrying grain, over the grain of
another to the damage of the neighbors or at any other
time." With holdings scattered and intermixed, roadways
and paths required strict regulation.

Another early fourteenth-century bylaw read: "Item,
that sheep shall not precede the larger animals"—that is,
plow oxen were to be pastured on the stubble of harvested
fields before the close-cropping sheep.

In the bylaws, the villagers met not as tenants of a lord
but as a democratic community. The regulations they
agreed on involved not their relationship to the lord but to
each other. The lord was affected by the bylaws only as
another landholder in the village, with a common interest
in the harvest and pasture. In the written records of the
bylaws found in the rolls of manorial courts, the lord was
seldom mentioned; instead the regulations were enacted by
the "community" or the "homage" or the "tenants" or the
"neighbors."

A characteristic institution of the manor was its court,
known in England as the *hallmote* or *halimote,* a place where
the lord dealt justice to his tenants, pocketing the fines. The
lowest court in the feudal hierarchy, it was also the chief
private court. Except in cases of murder or felony (tried by
royal courts), the manorial court had general jurisdiction
over all matters concerning the villagers. It took its name
from the lord's hall; it was a *moot* (Anglo-Saxon, "court")
that met in the hall, although actually it sometimes met in
the open air, under a traditional tree, or in the parish
church.

Presiding over the court was the lord's steward, but he
did not act as judge. His presence gave weight to the court's
decisions, but the verdicts, decided by the custom of the

manor, were rendered either by a jury of the court or by the whole body of its suitors. These were the men who owed attendance, or "suit," to the court, that is, the villeins of the manor and freeholders whose ancestors had owed suit, or who held land by a charter stipulating that they owed suit. Failure to attend meant a fine, unless the suitor sent someone with an excuse; the manorial court roll usually began with a list of the jurors, followed by a list of the excuses (*essoins*). The jurors, usually twelve in number, were chosen from the suitors. If a freeman was to be tried, a special jury of freemen seems to have been formed. In some villages the same men, a kind of aristocracy of jurymen, were chosen again and again.

The hallmote was more than a court of law; it handled many of the functions of the manorial government: the election and swearing in of manorial officials; payments for permission to marry, to enter the Church, to inherit a holding. When an heir succeeded to his father's land, a ceremony was enacted in the manorial court similar to that in which a king or baron invested the heir of a vassal with his lands. He received *seisin* (possession) of his holding "by the verge," which, as in the case of king or baron, dramatized the legal fiction that was the basis of relationship between lord and tenant: that the lord repossessed the holding and then regranted it to the heir, although inheritance was in fact fixed by custom. The steward held out a "verge" (stick) to the heir. When the heir took hold of the end of it, he was understood to have possession, as if the right flowed from steward to tenant along the stick.

Besides these official matters, the courts handled infractions of manorial customs concerning harvest, pasture, the maintaining of fences, and disputes among villagers over slanders, trespasses, boundaries, debts, and contracts. The usual punishment for a misdemeanor was a fine, sometimes in money, sometimes in workdays, which went to the lord.

Lawyers were not allowed in the manorial courts. Cases

were presented by the manorial officers concerned, or by the plaintiffs. In criminal cases, the steward might order the accused to find a certain number of men who would swear with him as a body that he was innocent of the misdeed with which he was charged. In a community where everyone knew his neighbor's business, if a man could find the necessary oath takers, he went free.

In civil cases, the procedure was by complaint. The plaintiff appeared before the court and complained that the defendant had injured him in such-and-such a way. The defendant could delay the case through a certain number of summonses, distraints, and excuses. Sometimes the plaintiff dropped the case. If he did so, however, he had to pay a fine, so that the lord did not have his court's time wasted. If the case did come to trial, the plaintiff opened with a statement of his plea, following traditional formulas, and the defendant replied, answering each item of the plea word for word, great stress being placed on the accuracy of wording. After both parties had been heard, judgment might be given by the jury, or by the whole court. The case was decided according to the facts and the custom: which of the two parties was believed to be telling the truth, and what was the custom of the manor. Sometimes the court decided that the suit was merely an expression of bad feeling, and the steward ordered the parties to hold a "love-day" before another hallmote at which they settled their differences and were reconciled.

Twice a year in some of the English counties, courts of the View of Frankpledge were held. In these districts all men twelve years and over were divided into groups of ten or twelve persons called frankpledges or tithings. The head of each tithing, the chief pledge, or tithingman, was usually elected for a year but often served for many years. Frankpledge was a police measure, a system by which a group of men was made responsible for the misdeeds of any of its members. Any malefactors in the group had to be brought to court, and the tithing could be fined for failure to do so. The twice-yearly inspection of the system known as the View of Frankpledge was originally held by the sheriff as a royal officer, but later, in many cases, it was usurped by the lords of manors as a source of income. It was also the occasion for the meeting of the most important manorial courts of the year, the Great Courts, which freeholders exempted from the ordinary hallmotes were compelled to attend, and where matters of local police and lesser cases of the Crown were presented.

The everyday relations of the villagers with the castle were governed by ancient custom and regulated by a group of officials at whose head was the lord's bailiff. The bailiff's duties on the lord's demesne land, as summed up in *Seneschaucie*, were manifold. He must survey the manor every morning—its woods, crops, meadows, and pastures; see that the plows were yoked; order the land marled and manured. He must watch over the threshers, the plowmen, the harrowers, and sowers; over the reaping and shocking, the sheep shearing, and the sale of wool and skins. He must inspect the lord's oxen, cows, heifers, and sheep, and weed out the old and weak, selling those that could not be maintained over the winter.

To the villagers the bailiff was the collector and enforcer —collector of rents and enforcer of labor services. Understandably, he was little loved. A fourteenth-century sermon told of a bailiff who, while riding to a village to collect rents, met the Devil in human form. The Devil asked, "Where are you going?" The bailiff replied, "To the next village, on my master's business." The Devil asked if he would take whatever was freely offered to him. The bailiff said Yes, and asked the questioner who he was and what was his business. The Devil replied that he was the Devil, busy like the bailiff in quest of gain, but willing "not to take *whatever* men would give me; but whatsoever they would gladly bestow with their whole heart and soul, that will I accept." "You do most justly," said the bailiff. As they approached the village, they saw a plowman angrily commending to the Devil his oxen that repeatedly strayed from the course. The bailiff said, "Behold, they are yours!" "No," said the Devil, "they are in no wise given from the heart." As they entered the village they heard a child weeping, and its mother wishing it to the Devil. Said the bailiff, "This is yours indeed!" "Not at all," said the Devil, "for she has no desire to lose her son." At length they reached the end of the village. A poverty-stricken widow whose only cow the bailiff had seized the day before saw him coming, and on her knees with hands outstretched shrieked at him, "To all the devils of hell I commend thee!" Whereupon the Devil exclaimed, "To be sure, this *is* mine. Because thus cordially you have been bestowed on me, I am willing to have you." And snatching up the bailiff, he bore him away to hell.

Under the bailiff a number of villagers held office both as servants of the lord and as village functionaries. The hayward—in charge of the *haie,* the hedge or fence—made sure that after fields were sowed the gaps in their hedges (usually "dead hedges" made of stakes and brushwood) were closed to keep out animals, and the fields were thus put "in defense." He also sometimes served as an officer of the hallmote, was part of the management of the lord's demesne farm, and impounded stray cattle. His badge of office was his horn, used to sound a warning that the cattle were in the corn (Little Boy Blue was a hayward). The woodward, who had charge of the lord's woods, was also a villager, elected by his fellows. In some villages there were also shepherds, swineherds, and oxherds, though often families had their own herdsmen. Although illiterate, the shepherds and haywards had no difficulty keeping accurate records of labor services, stock, expenditures of grain, and expenses. Their instrument was a stick, on which they cut notches that the reeve or bailiff translated into parchment records.

The reeve, the most important of the village officers, was commonly elected by the tenants from among their own number—"the best husbandman in the village," according to *Seneschaucie*. His responsibilities embraced every aspect of the manorial economy: overseeing all the activities of the villagers and the manorial servants, hailing them before the manorial court when they failed in their service, seeing to the upkeep of manorial buildings and implements and to the care of the lord's livestock. Himself intimately connected with the village, the reeve had an understanding of his neighbors that an outsider like the steward or bailiff could never have. This close relationship must also have added to the difficulties of his position, in which he belonged to the village while serving the lord. Although the reeve was usually released from all customary services, paid a stipend, and allowed to keep his horse in the lord's pasture and eat at the lord's table during the harvest, men often avoided the office if possible and even paid fines to be released from having to serve in it. When villages sent representatives to the royal courts, the reeve usually headed the delegation of four of the "best men" of the village.

The men of a medieval village were members of a parish which coincided with the village rather than the manor. The church was usually the only stone building of the village. On its altar stood the principal image of the saint to whom the church was dedicated. The rood (cross) over the entrance to the choir was lit by candles endowed by the pious.

The parish priest was supported partly by tithes—every tenth sheaf, or the crop of every tenth acre—partly by offerings on feast days, and partly by the *glebe,* land that belonged to the church and was tilled sometimes by tenants, sometimes by the priest himself. In many parts of England and Europe the "second-best beast" of every villein who died belonged to the priest. According to custom he returned a third of his revenues in alms and hospitality to

Reaping, with overseer. (Trustees of the British Museum. MS. 2 B.vii, f. 78v)

the poor, to repair the church, and to pay his chaplain or clerk, but abuse of the office was common. Often the holder of the benefice was an absentee who lived at the university or at court and hired a vicar to take his place. Sometimes an abbot or convent held the church and appointed a vicar. Poor vicars were often villeins whose fathers had paid the lord to allow them to enter the church. Such ill-educated clerics were sometimes accused of using their churches as barns, threshing corn in the nave, and pasturing cattle in the churchyard. Late in the thirteenth century Archbishop of Canterbury John Peckham was constrained to order parish priests to preach at least four times a year.

Despite its shortcomings, the parish church played an important part in the life of every villager. He worked in the fields to the sound of its bells, and though its Latin remained a mystery to him, he regularly attended Mass. The church's festivals marked the turning points of the year, and its rites every stage of a man's passage through life: birth, marriage, and death.

The ideal of the village community, where within each class opportunity was rendered equal, where neighbors worked together, where status and blood line were carefully preserved, century after century, endured for a long time. By contrast, the similar ideal of the medieval city dweller, toward which the craft guilds worked and legislated—every man practicing his craft and selling what he made, none very rich, none very poor—was only briefly and partially realized before the revival of commerce brought the rise of the great merchants and an increasing gap between rich and poor.

Much of the explanation for the greater durability of the village ideal lay in the slowness with which the money economy penetrated the countryside. Under the manorial system there was little scope for the kind of enterprise and industry that enriched the more successful city dwellers. Not until the sixteenth century did capitalist farmers appear in England, enclosing cultivated land, converting it to pasture, and changing tenants into wage laborers. Then, in the words of historian R. H. Tawney, "Villeinage ceases but the Poor Laws begin."

IX

The Making of
a Knight

When [Geoffrey of Anjou] entered the inner chamber of
the king's hall [at Rouen], surrounded by his knights and
those of the king and a crowd of people, the king . . . went to
meet him, affectionately embracing and kissing him, and,
taking him by the hand, led him to a seat . . . . All that day
was spent in joyful celebration. At the first dawn of the next
day, a bath was prepared, according to the custom for novice
knights . . . . After bathing, Geoffrey donned a linen under-
garment, a tunic of cloth of gold, a purple robe, silk
stockings, and shoes ornamented with golden lions; his
attendants, who were being initiated into knighthood with
him, also put on gold and purple. [Geoffrey], with his train of
nobles, left the chamber to appear in public. Horses and
arms were brought and distributed. A Spanish horse of
wonderful beauty was provided for Geoffrey, swifter than the
flight of birds. He was then armed with a corselet of
double-woven mail which no lance or javelin could pierce,
and shod with iron boots of the same double mesh; golden

spurs were girded on; a shield with golden lions was hung around his neck; a helmet was placed on his head gleaming with many precious stones, and which no sword could pierce or mar; a spear of ash tipped with iron was provided; and finally from the royal treasury was brought an ancient sword . . . . Thus our novice knight was armed, the future flower of knighthood, who despite his armor leapt with marvelous agility on his horse. What more can be said? That day, dedicated to the honor of the newly made knights, was spent entirely in warlike games and exercises. For seven whole days the celebration in honor of the new knights continued.

Thus, in the description of chronicler Jean of Tours, was fifteen-year-old Geoffrey of Anjou initiated into knighthood by his future father-in-law, Henry I, in 1128. To the secular ritual the later twelfth century added a religious element. The aspirant kept a nightlong vigil in the castle chapel, purifying his soul as the bath cleansed his body. At daybreak a priest celebrated mass, after which the youth joined family and friends for breakfast. He then dressed in new clothes made especially for the occasion, usually of pure white rather than the purple-and-gold of Geoffrey of Anjou—white silk shirt, trunks, and tunic, and an ermine robe.

The dubbing ceremony commonly took place in the open air, on a platform or carpet, amid flourishes of trumpets and the music of minstrels. The youth's father and several other knights, often including the father's lord, helped him with his armor and equipment. The sword, blessed the night before by the priest, was brought; the young man reverently kissed its hilt, in the hollow of which holy relics might be encased.

Now came the climax, the *colée,* or buffet, usually executed by the father. Far from being a gently symbolic blow, the *colée* was an open-handed whack that often

Knighting. The novice is girded with a sword. (Trustees of the British Museum)

knocked its recipient, prepared though he was, off his feet. According to the Spanish writer Ramon Lull, the purpose of the *colée* was an aid to memory, so that the young knight would not forget his oath, now administered.

"Go, fair son! Be a true knight, and courageous in the face of your enemies," says the father in one romance. "Be thou brave and upright, that God may love thee—and remember that thou springest from a race that can never be false," says another. The young man replies, "So shall I, with God's help!"

The ceremony over, the new-made knight sometimes entered the church and placed his sword on the altar, in sign of its dedication to the Holy Church.

He was now a knight, a member of the order of chivalry. His war horse, a gift of his father or lord, was led up in full harness. As soon as he was in the saddle, the young man was given his lance and shield, and after a gallop about, attacked the quintain, a dummy fashioned of chain mail covered with a shield and set on a post. Sometimes there was more than one post for the new knight to knock down, to make the test more difficult and more interesting. The show was usually topped off with mock fighting with lance and shield.

On occasion, knights were dubbed on the battlefield. William Marshal was knighted in 1167 by his sponsor and older cousin, William of Tancarville, hereditary chamberlain of Normandy, during the war between Henry II and Louis VII of France. On his way with reinforcements for the count of Eu at Drincourt, the chamberlain summoned the Norman barons under his command for the ceremony. Dressed in a new mantle, William Marshal stood before his cousin, who "girt him with a sword" and gave him the *colée*. Several years later, in 1173, William Marshal similarly knighted young Henry, Henry II's eldest son, as preparation for battle. Henry handed the sword to William, saying, "I wish this honor to come from God and from you," and in the presence of Henry's entourage and assembled barons and knights, William "girt on the sword." Instead of a buffet, William bestowed a kiss on the young man, "and," in the words of William's biographer, "so he was a knight." More than four decades later William knighted another royal personage, nine-year-old Henry III, on the eve of his coronation.

Originally the term *chevalier* (*caballero, cavaliere, Ritter*—the

Tilting at the quintain. (Bodleian Library. MS. Bod. 264, f. 82v)

word in all languages, except the English "knight," means horseman) simply indicated a warrior who fought on horseback, but even in its earliest stage it connoted a superiority of class, since only a man of means could afford a horse. The foundation of the crusading Order of the Temple in the twelfth century contributed both to the formalization of knighthood and to its association with Christianity. A Knight Templar wore a distinctive white-mantled uniform and swore to live by a Rule drawn from the Augustinian and Benedictine monks.

Thus the knight was a member of the noble class socially through the profession of arms, economically through the possession of horse and armor, and officially through a ceremony imbued with a religious sanction.

The origin of the knight's horse (destrier, charger) remains something of a mystery. Apparently bred from partly Arab stock, he was huge and strong, capable of sustaining the shock combat that had revolutionized warfare. Through no coincidence, northwest France, the cradle of feudalism, was noted for its horse breeding. The later Percheron and Belgian draft horses (as well as the Suffolk in England) were descended from the medieval destriers.

As clashes between armed and mounted knights multiplied and as the Italian-introduced crossbow was adopted, improvements in armor became necessary, made possible by the growing affluence of the twelfth century. The conical, open-faced helmet of the First Crusade was replaced by a massive pot helmet that covered head, face, and neck, while the old-fashioned hauberk (shirt of mail), made of small metal discs sewn on linen, turned into chain mail, composed of interlocking iron rings and weighing forty pounds or more. (Plate armor still lay far in the future.)

Through the twelfth century the tendency toward exclusivity grew in the knightly class. Frederick Barbarossa and probably other sovereigns forbade peasants to become knights or to carry sword or lance, and by the thirteenth century the knightly aristocracy was in theory a closed caste, set apart from the rest of society. "Ah, God! how badly is the good warrior rewarded who makes the son of a villein a knight!" warns the romance *Girart de Roussillon*. But the poet's admonition is itself evidence that villeins did indeed become knights in the twelfth century, and in the thirteenth the process was almost commonplace. The chief reason was the growing wealth of the merchant class. A grandfather might found a business, a father expand it, a son inherit a fortune. Such a son might purchase estates in the country from which he could draw an aristocratic name; he could afford expensive entertainment and bribes to great lords, and be knighted if he chose. Thenceforward his descendants were knights. Rather than seeking to suppress the custom, the great lords, in defiance of such edicts as Barbarossa's, took the sensible course of regularizing it by charging a fixed fee for knighthood.

At the other end of the economic scale, again despite all prohibitions to the contrary, many a poor soldier won knighthood through valor in the service of a lord. Despite this double-ended openness of the knightly class, it nevertheless retained a distinct caste rigidity. Its newest members,

The baron's blacksmith shapes a helmet on his anvil while an assistant tests a sword with his eye and servants wait with another helmet and a horse wearing chain-mail armor. (Trinity College, Cambridge. MS. 0.9.34, f. 24r)

like parvenus of every age, copied or even excelled the hauteur of their older brothers in aristocracy.

Whatever his father's origin, the son of a knight normally grew up to be knighted. As a squire, or knight-aspirant, he began his apprenticeship, often in the household of his father's lord, cleaning out stables, currying horses, cleaning armor, serving at table, while he learned to ride a horse and wield sword and lance, with plenty of practice at the quintain. William Marshal underwent this training for eight years in the household of William of Tancarville.

The youthful aspirant was thoroughly imbued with the code of chivalry. In the twelfth and thirteenth centuries the chivalric ideal was fostered by the legends that had grown up around Charlemagne and Roland, and in England by the newer King Arthur stories. Arthur, a barely discernible real-life figure in sixth-century Britain (as was Roland in ninth-century France) was first given prominence in the

Military training

twelfth century by Geoffrey of Monmouth in his highly imaginative *History of the Kings of Britain*. Robert Wace, a Norman poet from the island of Jersey, read Geoffrey's book and made Arthur the hero of a romance he composed for Eleanor of Aquitaine. Wace embellished Arthur's court with a Round Table, and Chrétien de Troyes, a poet at the court of Eleanor's daughter Marie of Champagne, moved Arthur's court from Caerleon, Monmouthshire, to fictitious (or undetermined) Camelot. Chrétien's romances completed an important transition by shifting emphasis from Arthur himself to the knights, especially Lancelot and Percival. Chrétien and other poets, English, French, and German, glorified the code by which knights were supposed to live, stressing honor, generosity, loyalty, and dedication to God and Church.

The castle lord who dubbed Percival, depicted as a naive young savage from Wales, told him:

> With this sword [I have given you] the highest Order
> That God has made and commanded:
> It is the Order of Chivalry
> Which should be without taint [vilenie].

Percival was admonished to spare the vanquished enemy who asked grace, to assist maidens and women in distress, to pray in church regularly, and not to talk too much—this last evidently a reflection on the knightly inclination to boast.

Many thirteenth-century knights, including William Marshal, themselves composed verses. It was a poor knight who could not read and write. One romance credits its noble young hero with learning Latin and astronomy from a tutor who "attended his pupil everywhere, took him to school, prevented him from eating too much, taught him polite language and good manners, and never left him even when he dressed or went to bed."

Despite precepts, codes, and admonitions from the Church, however, the knight's life was normally lived on a lower plane than that embodied by the chivalric ideal. The reason was that the great majority of knights were, horse and armor aside, penniless. The system of primogeniture left younger sons even of great families without fiefs, and so without income. These young men were sent out into the world with the training and equipment for a single profession, that of arms. The normal business of the knight was war, and often as a mercenary. By the twelfth century, the practice of hiring knights was well established, and even if a knight served his liege lord as part of a feudal levy, the thought of gain was in the forefront of his mind. One of young William Marshal's first lessons, immediately following his initiation into battle at Drincourt, was an exercise in economics. That night at dinner, William of Mandeville, earl of Essex, who had shared command with the chamberlain during the battle, ironically asked William for a small present out of his spoils—"just a crupper or an old horse-collar . . . surely you won forty or sixty horses today?" Embarrassed, William had to admit that not only had he failed to seize the opportunity of booty, but he had even lost his own horse. A few days later there was a tournament that William, horseless, could not enter. At the last moment William's tutor provided him with a horse. The young man fought three victorious combats, and took care to exact horses, arms, armor, baggage, and ransom money.

Many years later William Marshal, as regent for young Henry III, defeated Prince Louis of France and rebel English barons at Lincoln. Roger of Wendover, in his chronicle *Flowers of History*, reports that William allowed his men to do much more than seize enemy horses and treasure-laden wagons:

> The whole city was plundered to the last farthing, and then they proceeded to rob all the churches throughout the city, breaking open all the chests and cupboards with hatchets and hammers, and seizing gold and silver, cloth of all colors, women's ornaments, gold rings, goblets, and precious stones. When at last they had carried off all kinds of merchandise so that nothing remained untouched in any corner of the houses, they all returned to their own lords rich men. When the peace of King Henry had been proclaimed throughout the city by all, they feasted and drank and made merry.

The Provençal poet Bertrand de Born wrote lyrically about war—its pageantry, its excitement, and its booty:

> . . . I love to see,
> Amid the meadows, tents and pavilions spread out,
> And it gives me great joy to see
> Drawn up on the field
> Knights and horses in battle array,
> And it delights me when the scouts
> Scatter people and herds in their path . . . .
> Maces, swords, helms of different colors,
> Shields that will be riven and shattered
> When the fight begins;
> Many vassals struck down together,
> And the horses of the dead and wounded
> Roving at random . . . .
> I tell you I find no such savor
> In food, or in wine, or in sleep,
> As in hearing the shout "On! On!"
> From both sides, and the neighing of steeds

That have lost their riders,
And the cries of "Help! Help!"
In seeing men great and small go down
On the grass beyond the castle moat;
In seeing at last the dead,
The pennoned stumps of lances
Still in their sides.

Bertrand, who personally stirred up so much strife
between great feudal lords that Dante awarded him a
special place in Hell, with his head permanently severed
from his body, was explicit about the material reasons for
"finding no pleasure in peace":

> Why do I want
> The rich to hate each other?
> Because a rich man is much more
> Noble, generous and affable
> In war than in peace.

And again:

> We are going to have some fun.
> For the barons will make much of us . . . .
> If they want us to remain with them,
> They will give us money.
> To the soldier's pay will be added loot:
> Trumpet, drums, flags and pennons,
> Standards of horses white and black—
> This is what we shall shortly see.
> And it will be a happy day,
> For we shall seize the usurers' goods,
> And pack animals will no longer pass in safety,
> Or the burgher journey without fear,
> Or the merchant on his way to France,
> But the man full of courage will be rich.

Addressing himself to the count of Poitiers, Bertrand offered
his services: "I can help you. I have already a shield at my
neck and a helm on my head . . . . Nevertheless, how can
I put myself in the field without money?"

A similarly enthusiastic attitude toward war was expressed by a Welsh chronicler describing a campaign of Prince Llywelyn in 1220 in which he stormed and razed two castles, burned the town of Haverford, and "went round Rhos and Deugleddyv in five days, making vast slaughter of the people of the country. And after making a truce . . . he returned home happy and joyful."

Of all sources of knightly enrichment, the ransom of wealthy prisoners was the foremost. Following a battle in the *chanson* of *Girart de Roussillon,* Girart and his followers casually put to the sword all their penniless prisoners, but spared the "owners of castles." Ransom of an important personage could reach astronomical figures—like the "king's ransom" of Richard I when he was captured by Leopold of Austria and turned over to Emperor Henry VI: 150,000 marks (several million dollars in twentieth-century American currency), which had to be raised by special taxes levied in both England and Normandy, on knights, laymen, clergy, churches, monasteries. The sum could not be raised, and when Richard was freed, he had to give hostages for the remaining debt.

In France the peace established in the thirteenth century under Louis IX left many knights without a field of action. Numbers of them went to the East as members of the two Crusading orders, the Temple and the Hospital; others went to Spain and Portugal. Their intention was, of course, to fight the Saracen infidels, but it did not always work out that way. Even the Cid, epic hero of Spanish chivalry, spent considerable time in the employ of the infidels, leading expeditions for the Moorish king of Saragossa against Christian princes. For poor knights dependent on their swords for their livelihood, one employer was as good as another. *Girart de Roussillon* paints a sad picture of the knight when peace has come—his income cut off, and the money-lender after him. Girart and his wife, roaming the countryside, meet some merchants restored to prosperity by the peace that has ruined Girart. They find it prudent to conceal Girart's identity, and his wife tells the merchants he is dead. "God be praised," says one, "for he was always making war and through him we have suffered many ills." Frustrated Girart wishes he could cut the fellow down with one blow of his good sword, but he no longer has it.

In the lean times of peace there remained one source of action and possible gain: the tournament. Historically an outgrowth of old pagan games, taken over like so many other pagan institutions by the early Middle Ages and accorded a Christian coloration, the tournament had by the thirteenth century evolved its own rules and formalities. Great lords and princes organized tournaments for their own entertainment and that of their friends, and to show off their wealth. The principal feature was a mock battle between groups of knights from different regions. Heralds were sent around the countryside to proclaim the tournament, and on the appointed day the knights donned their armor, mounted their horses, and lined up at opposite ends of a level meadow. At a flourish from a herald, the two bands of horsemen charged at each other. The field was open-ended, because when one team was defeated and sought to retreat, the other, exactly as in real war, pursued it through wood and dale to capture prisoners. When it was all over, the defeated knights had to arrange with their captors for their ransom, usually the value of horse and armor, redeemed by a money payment. William Marshal and another knight made a two-year tour of France attending tournaments, in one ten-month period capturing 103 knights and doing a profitable business in ransoms.

There were also prizes, sometimes for several categories of prowess. William Marshal once won a fish, a pike of unusual size. The knights who delivered it found William at the blacksmith's, down on his knees, his head on the anvil, while the smith labored to release him from his helmet, which had gotten turned around backwards from a lance's blow.

Until the latter part of the fourteenth century, there was little individual jousting. The tournament was essentially training for war, and the mass melee intentionally resembled a real battle. The combative ardor of the participants was often very akin to the spirit of genuine war, especially if knightly loyalties were enlisted. Serious and even fatal injuries were common. At one tournament William Marshal's son Gilbert was exhibiting his skill at horsemanship when the bridle broke. Gilbert was tumbled from the saddle and, catching one foot in the stirrup, was dragged across the field and fatally injured. After the accident, the tournament degenerated into a brawl in which one of Gilbert's retainers was killed and many knights and squires were badly wounded. A decade later a tournament near Rochester ended with English squires belaboring the defeated French knights with sticks and clubs.

The earliest English tournaments had been licensed by the king, but Henry III consistently opposed them. William Marshal forbade one in Henry's name in 1217, and thereafter the prohibitions multiplied, but they were so ineffectual that according to the monastic chronicler of the *Annals of Dunstable*, "tourneyers, their aiders and abettors, and those who carried merchandise or provisions to tournaments were ordered to be excommunicated, all together, regularly every Sunday."

The tournament at which Gilbert Marshal was killed had been forbidden by the king—a fact which Henry pointed out to Walter Marshal when the latter claimed his brother's inheritance: "And you too, Walter, who against my wish and notwithstanding my prohibition, and in contempt of me, were present at the tournament . . . on what grounds do you demand your inheritance?" Walter's protests that he could not leave his brother did not soften the king's anger, but the intercession of the bishop of Durham finally brought about a reconciliation.

Aside from the fear that the king expressed when he canceled two tournaments in 1247 between knights of his own French province of Poitou and those of his English domain (he was afraid, in the words of Matthew Paris, that "after the spears were shivered, bloody swords might flash forth"), Henry III regarded tournaments as pretexts for conspiracy by the barons. In several cases these mock wars were closely connected with baronial uprisings. On the occasion of an abortive rising at Stamford in 1229 after Henry's coming of age, the barons involved rode off to Chepstow with William Marshal II for a tournament, only to be confronted with a writ by the justiciar, Hubert de Burgh, forbidding the meeting. Seventy-three more prohibitions were recorded in the ensuing three decades. Several times knights holding tournaments had their lands seized. On one occasion the king's brother, William de Valence, urged his knightly companions to defy the king's order and hold a tournament, which was only prevented by a heavy fall of snow. A little later William staged the tournament and succeeded in severely wounding a fellow knight.

The Church joined Henry in its opposition, not only because of the violence of the combats and the danger of sedition. Besides such innocent auxiliary sports as wrestling, dart shooting, lance hurling, and stone throwing, the tournaments were famous for eating, drinking, and love-making. Jacques de Vitry, the Paris preacher renowned for the acerbity of his sermons, liked to use the tournament to illustrate all seven of the deadly sins. The Church's strictures were not very effective. Jocelin of Brakelond records how Abbot Samson of Bury St. Edmunds forbade a band of young knights to hold a tournament and went so far as to lock the town gates to keep them from the field. Next day, on the Feast of Peter and Paul, the young men foreswore combat and came to dine with the abbot. But after dinner, sending for more wine, they caroused, sang, ruined the abbot's afternoon nap, and finally marched out, broke open the town gates, and held their tournament. The abbot excommunicated the lot.

In the 1250s a milder form of combat, known in England as a Round Table (named after King Arthur's assemblies), anticipated the tournaments of the fourteenth and fifteenth centuries, replacing the mass melee with adversaries in single combat with blunted weapons. Such meetings were usually preceded by feasting and games. But even the Round Tables could be lethal. In 1252 Matthew Paris recorded the death of Arnold de Montigny in a joust with Roger de Lemburn, which brought suspicion of murder because the iron point of Roger's lance, when drawn from the dead man's throat, was found not to have been blunted as it should have been. Further, Roger had previously wounded Arnold in a tournament. Matthew concluded, "But God only knows the truth of this, who alone searches into the secrets of men's hearts."

At another Round Table in 1256, held at Blyth, the seventeen-year-old Prince Edward fought in armor of linen cloth and with light weapons; but the meeting, like the mass melees, ended in turmoil, with the participants beaten and trampled on. According to Matthew Paris, a number of nobles, including Earl Marshal Roger Bigod of Chepstow, "never afterwards recovered their health." Prince Edward, as Edward I, sought to regulate rather than ban tournaments and Round Tables. His statute of 1267 aimed at preventing riots by limiting the number of squires and specifying the weapons carried by knights, squires, grooms, footmen, heralds, and spectators. At Edward's own royal tourneys, there were no casualties.

In France the melee gave way to the joust even earlier. Tournaments of the later type are depicted by the authors of the romances as brave and colorful pageants. In the *Castellan of Coucy*, the heralds appeared at an early hour to awaken the many guests who had arrived at the castle:

Mass sung and the ladies installed in the pavilions, the jousts began without delay. The first was between the Duke of Limbourg and a bachelor named Gautier de Soul, who broke three lances apiece without losing the stirrups . . . . The seventh was one of the most powerful shows of arms and the most pleasant to see: the first champion wore a sleeve [a token of his lady] on his right arm, and when he went to his station, the heralds cried, "Coucy, Coucy, the brave man, the valiant bachelor, the Castellan of Coucy!" Against him appeared successively Gaucher of Chatillon and Count Louis of Blois . . . . Two more jousts took place; then night fell and the assembly separated to La Fère and Vendeuil . . . . The next day the jousts continued [until] only three knights were left, the others all being wounded . . . . At the first pass the Castellan knocked down his adversary's helmet into the dust, and blood ran from his mouth and nose . . . . On the third try both men were disarmed and fell unconscious to the ground. Valets, sergeants and squires laid them on their shields and carried them from the field . . . . But it was only, thank God, a passing unconsciousness; neither man was dead. Everyone thanked God and the saints.

Then the Sire de Coucy invited the knights and ladies to dine . . . . More than twenty tents were set up between the Oise and the forest, in fields full of flowers. The Sire de Coucy and all the Vermandois were dressed in green samite studded with golden eagles; they came to the tents leading by the finger the ladies of their country. The men of Hainaut and their ladies were dressed in gold embroidered with black lions; they arrived singing, two by two. The Champenois, the Burgundians, the men of Berri, were also in uniform, scarlet samite decorated with golden leopards.

The tournament gave an impetus to one of the best-known traditions of feudalism and knighthood—the art of heraldry, which took its name from the fact that tournament heralds became experts in the design of heraldic devices. Symbols on banners and shields to distinguish leaders in the melee of a feudal battle were common as early as the eleventh century. The Bayeux Tapestry shows such devices for both Harold and William. In the twelfth century the custom grew of passing on the device from father to son, like the shield with the golden lions which Geoffrey of Anjou received at his knighting from his father-in-law, Henry I, an emblem inherited by Geoffrey's grandson William Longespée, earl of Salisbury. Another early device was that of the Clare family, lords of Chepstow; in about 1140 Gilbert de Clare adopted three chevrons, similar to those later used in military insignia. The Clare arms appeared on the lord's shield, and probably flew from Chepstow to signal the owner's presence in his castle. Crests, in the form of three-dimensional figures—a boar, a lion, a hawk—were added to the helmet as early as the end of the twelfth century.

In the thirteenth century, the functional value of the heraldic device, or coat of arms, as it came to be called from its use on surcoats, was strongly reinforced as chivalric ideology became popular and affluence encouraged the decorative arts. Even more important was its character as a badge of nobility, visually setting its owner apart from the common people (although wealthy townsmen continued to acquire knightly status and coats of arms to authenticate it). From art, heraldry progressed to become a science, with its own rigid rules and its own jargon. Shields could be partitioned into segments only in certain specified ways, such as *tierced in fesse* (divided into three horizontally) or *in saltire* (cut into four portions by a diagonal cross). Dragons, lions, leopards, eagles, fish, and many other animals, including mythological ones, were used, besides stars, moons, trees, bushes, flowers, and other objects both natural and man-made. The addition of a motto came into fashion, like the French kings' *Montjoye,* the rallying cry and standard of Charlemagne in the *Chanson de Roland*. All the elements of the arms—crest, helmet, shield, and motto—were finally assembled in a standardized form of heraldic device.

A custom of English nobles that may date to the thirteenth century, that of hanging their heraldic banners outside inns where they were staying, led to the inn sign of later times: the White Hart from the badge of Richard II, the Swan from that of the earls of Hereford, the Rose and Crown from the badge of England.

In the thirteenth century the institution of knighthood, closely related to the life of the castle, was perhaps at its zenith. Already, in fact, signs of decadence were evident in the growing sophistication of attitudes. The *Chanson de Roland*, written at about the time of the First Crusade, and in which the word "chivalrous" makes its first appearance, breathes a spirit of rugged Christian naiveté. Roland brings disaster on Charlemagne's rear guard by refusing to sound his horn and let Charlemagne know the Saracens are attacking, because to call for help would be cowardly. "Better death than dishonor," is Roland's view. His strategy is simple: "Strike with your lance," he tells Oliver, "and I will smite with Durendal, my good sword which the emperor gave me. If I die, he who shall inherit it will say: it was the sword of a noble vassal." Durendal contains in its hilt, among other sacred relics, a scrap of the Virgin's garment. After a terrific battle in which Saracens are cut down in windrows while the French knights drop one by one, the dying Roland is left alone on the corpse-strewn field, his last thoughts of his two lords, Charlemagne and God, to whom he holds his glove aloft as he expires.

The chivalric ideal of the *Chanson de Roland*, developed and celebrated by the poets of the twelfth century, embraced generosity, honor, the pursuit of glory, and contempt for hardship, fatigue, pain, and death.

But by the thirteenth century it was possible to write a

totally different kind of book on the same theme of crusading against the Saracens. The *Histoire de Saint-Louis*, by the Sieur de Joinville, seneschal of Champagne, presents a striking contrast to *Roland*. The chronicle of the ill-fated crusade of Louis IX to Egypt tells in honest prose a story not dissimilar to that of *Roland*—Christian French knights fighting bravely against heavy odds and in the end nearly all dying. But the difference in tone is vast: Joinville's knights are real, they suffer from their wounds and disease, and death seems more miserable than glorious. And even though Joinville cherishes and admires the saintly Louis much as Roland loved Charlemagne, his attitude is very different. St. Louis asks Joinville, "Which would you prefer: to be a leper or to have committed some mortal sin?" The honest seneschal reports, "I, who had never lied to him, replied that I would rather have committed thirty mortal sins than become a leper."

Common sense has intruded on chivalry.

X

The Castle at War

WARFARE IN THE MIDDLE AGES centered around castles. The clumsy, disorganized feudal levies, called out for a few weeks' summer service, rarely met in pitched battles. Their most efficient employment was in sieges, a condition that fitted neatly into the capital strategic value of the castle.

Medieval warfare was not as incessant as some of the older historians have pictured it. The motte-and-bailey stronghold of the ninth and tenth centuries was frequently embroiled, either with Viking, Saracen, and Hungarian marauders or with neighboring barons, but by the eleventh century the marauders had been discouraged and private warfare was on the wane. In England it was outlawed by William the Conqueror and effectively suppressed by his successors. To take its place there were the Crusades, including those against Spanish Moors and French Albigensians; international wars, such as those waged by Richard the Lionhearted, John and Henry III in France, and the wars of conquest in Wales, Scotland, and Ireland; and civil wars, such as that fought by Stephen of Blois and the Empress Matilda over the throne, and the numerous rebellions of barons against royal authority. Despite all these, many twelfth- and thirteenth-century castles were rarely besieged, and Chepstow was unusual but by no means unique in passing entirely through the Middle Ages without ever seeing an enemy at its gates.

Nevertheless, when war broke out, it inevitably revolved around castles. Enemy castles were major political-military objectives in themselves, and many were sited specifically to bar invasion routes. Typically the castle stood on high ground commanding a river crossing, a river confluence, a stretch of navigation, a coastal harbor, a mountain pass, or some other strategically important feature. The castle inside a city could be defended long after the city had been taken, and an unsubdued castle garrison could sally out and reoccupy the town the moment the enemy left. Even a rural castle could not safely be bypassed, because its garrison could cut the invader's supply lines. The mobility of the garrison—nearly always supplied with horses—conferred a large strategic radius for many purposes: raiding across a border, furnishing a supply base for an army on the offensive, interrupting road or river traffic at a distance. For all these reasons, medieval military science was the science of the attack and defense of castles.

The castle's main line of resistance was the curtain wall with its projecting towers. The ground in front of the curtain was kept free of all cover; if there was a moat, the ground was cleared well beyond it. Where the approach to the castle was limited by the site, and especially where it was limited to one single direction, the defenses on the vulnerable side multiplied, with combinations of walls, moats, and towers masking the main curtain wall. At Chepstow the eastern end was protected by the Great

Gatehouse, with its arrow loops, portcullises, and machicolations. The barbican built by the Marshals to protect the
western end consisted of a walled enclosure a hundred feet
wide by fifty deep, with a powerful cylindrical tower at the
southwest corner and a fortified gatehouse on the northwest.
The barbican was separated from the west curtain wall by a
broad ditch, or dry moat, crossed by a bridge with a draw
span and overlooked by a strong rectangular tower on the
inner side. The ditch ended at the south wall in an
inconspicuous postern which, even if forced, would admit
the enemy only to a trap, enfiladed by the towers and the
wall parapet. The long sides of the castle had strong natural
defenses: the river with its high bluff on the north, and the
steep slope of the ridge on the south toward the town.

Such a castle as Chepstow was practically proof against
direct assault, while its size provided ample facilities for
storing provisions. Some castles kept a year's supply of food
or even more on hand, and the relatively small size of a
thirteenth-century garrison often meant that in a prolonged
siege the assailants rather than the besieged were confronted with a supply problem. A garrison of sixty men
could hold out against an attacking force ten times its
number, and feeding sixty men from a well-stocked granary
supplemented by cattle, pigs, and chickens brought in at the
enemy's approach might be far easier than feeding 600 men
from a war-ravaged countryside.

By the late thirteenth century, castle logistics were on a
sophisticated basis, with supplies often purchased from
general contractors, such as the consignments ordered from
one John Hutting in June 1266 to supply the castle of
Rochester, used as a base by Henry III's general Roger
Leyburn: 251 herrings, 50 sheep, 51 salted pigs, and
quantities of figs, rice, and raisins. More commonly a single
commodity was bought from an individual merchant or
group of merchants; for Rochester, Roger Leyburn bought
fish from merchants of Northfleet and Strood; oats from

Military provision carts carrying helmets and hauberks, cooking pots hung along the sides. (Maciejowski Bible, Pierpont Morgan Library. MS. 638, f. 27v)

Maidstone, Leeds, and Nessindon; rye from a merchant of Colchester, and wine from Peter of London and Henry the Vintner of Sittingbourne.

A castle's water supply frequently offered a more vulnerable target than its food supply. Although a reliable well, in or near the keep, was one of the basic necessities of a castle, wells sometimes failed, and when they did the results were disastrous. In the First Crusade, when the Turks besieged the Crusaders in the castle of Xerigordo near Nicaea and cut off their water supply, the beleaguered Christians suffered terrific hardships, drinking their horses' blood and each other's urine, and burying themselves in damp earth in hope of absorbing the moisture. After eight days without water the Christians surrendered, and were killed or sold as slaves. Two decades later Count Fulk of Anjou, besieging

Henry I's castle of Alençon, managed to locate and destroy an underground conduit from the river Sarthe, and the garrison was forced to surrender. In 1136, when King Stephen was besieging a rebellious baron, Baldwin of Redvers, in the castle of Exeter, the castle's two wells suddenly went dry. The garrison drank wine as long as it lasted, also using it to make bread, to cook, and to put out fires set by the attackers. In the end the rebels yielded, and, in the words of the chronicler of the *Gesta Stephani*, "when they finally came forth you could have seen the body of each individual wasted and enfeebled with parching thirst, and once they were outside they hurried rather to drink a draught of any sort than to discharge any business whatsoever."

Hunger and thirst aside, no defensive fortification was proof against all attack, and even the strongest castles of the twelfth and thirteenth centuries could be, and were, captured. The castle had few vulnerable points, but what few it had were assiduously exploited by its enemies.

A frequent structural weakness of castles lay in their subsoil. Unless a castle was founded wholly on solid rock, some part of its walls could be undermined by digging. The procedure was to drive a tunnel beneath the wall, preferably under a corner or tower, supporting the tunnel roof with heavy timbers as the sappers advanced. When they reached a point directly under the wall, the timbering was set ablaze, collapsing earth and masonry above. The process was not as easy as it sounds. In 1215, when King John laid siege to Rochester Castle, a vast twelfth-century square keep defended by about a hundred rebel knights and a number of foot soldiers and bowmen, he ordered nearby Canterbury to manufacture "by day and night as many picks as you are able." Six weeks later the digging had progressed to the point when John commanded justiciar Hubert de Burgh to "send to us with all speed by day and night forty of the fattest pigs of the sort least good for eating

Erecting a tent. On the left, a foot-soldier raises a pole, while another drives in the stakes and a third holds the rope. (Trustees of the British Museum. MS. Lans. 782, f. 34v)

to bring fire beneath the tower." The lard produced a sufficient blaze in the mine to destroy the timbering and bring down a great section of the wall of the keep.

A castle built on a solid rock foundation, such as Chepstow, had to be attacked with two other main devices inherited by medieval military engineers from ancient predecessors: the mobile assault tower and the siege engine or catapult artillery. The assault tower, usually called a cat, but sometimes a bear or other figurative term, was normally assembled from components brought to the site. The aim of all the many designs was to provide the storming party with cover and height, neutralizing the advantages of the defenders. The tower might be employed to seize a section of the rampart or to provide cover for sappers or a battering ram. The immense gates of the powerful castles of the High Middle Ages were rarely forced by ramming, though a small castle might be vulnerable to the heavy beam or tree trunk, fronted with an iron or copper head (sometimes literally a ram's head), either grasped directly by its crew or swung from leather thongs. Before any form of direct assault, the moat defense had first to be dealt with, usually by filling it in with brush and earth. The assault tower, containing both archers and assault troops to engage the defenders hand-to-hand, could then be wheeled forward to the castle wall. A large besieging army could build and man several such towers and by attacking different points of the wall exploit its numerical advantage. Since the towers were wooden, the castle's defenders tried to set them afire by hurling torches or fire-bearing arrows.

Medieval engineers used the ancient tension and torsion engines, in the commonest form of which a tightly wound horizontal skein, its axis parallel to the wall under attack, was wound still tighter by an upright timber arm fixed to its shaft at right angles, and drawn back to ground level. The timber arm, or firing beam, now under great tension, was charged with a missile at its extreme end and released. At the upright position the arm's leap forward was halted by a padded crossbar, causing the missile to fly on. Data on ranges are scarce, but modern experiments have achieved a distance of 200 yards with 50-pound rocks.

Medieval engineers devised another form, the trebuchet, driven by a counterweight, an invention also used for castle drawbridges. The Arabs had used a catapult in which the beam was pulled down by a gang of men and released. European military engineers introduced a decisive improvement. In the trebuchet, the firing beam was pivoted on a crosspole about a quarter of its length from its butt end, which was pointed at the enemy castle. The butt end was

A battering ram.

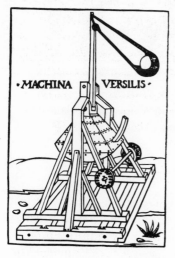

A trebuchet.

weighted with a number of measured weights calibrated for range, and the long end, pulled down by means of a winch, was loaded with the missile. Released, the beam sprang to the upright position, discharging the missile with a power and accuracy said to be superior to that of the tension and torsion engines. First used in Italy at the end of the twelfth century, the trebuchet was widely employed in the Albigensian Crusade of the early 1200s. It made its appearance

Battle scene from the thirteenth-century Maciejowski Bible. Top left, loading a trebuchet; adjustable counterweights are hidden behind the melee at the center of the picture. (Pierpont Morgan Library. MS. 638, f. 23v)

in England in 1216 during the siege of Dover by Prince Louis of France. The following year a trebuchet was carried on one of Louis's ships when his fleet, attempting to enter the mouth of the Thames, was decisively defeated in the battle of Sandwich; the machine weighed down the ship "so deep in the water that the deck was almost awash," and proved a handicap rather than an advantage in the encounter. The effectiveness of the trebuchet in a siege was formidable, however, because of its capacity to hit the same target repeatedly with precision. In 1244 Bishop Durand of Albi designed a trebuchet for the siege of Montségur that hurled a succession of missiles weighing forty kilograms (eighty-eight pounds) at the same point in the wall day and night, at twenty-minute intervals, until it battered an opening.

Ammunition of the attackers included inflammables for firing the timber buildings of the castle bailey. The effectiveness of stone projectiles depended on the height and thickness of the stone walls against which they were flung. The walls of the early twelfth century could be battered down, and often were. The result was the construction of much heavier walls—in Windsor Castle, for example, reaching a thickness of twenty-four feet.

Defenders of large castles used artillery of their own for counter-battery fire. During Edward I's Welsh wars, an engineer named Reginald added four *springalds* (catapults) to the towers of Chepstow, one mounted on William Fitz Osbern's keep. Trebuchets and mangonels, mounted on the towers or even on the broad walls of castles, hurled rocks, frequently the besiegers' own back at them, with the additional advantage gained from height.

A different principle—that of the crossbow—supplied another form of artillery for both besiegers and besieged. The ancient Roman ballista, easy to mount on castle walls, discharged a giant arrow, or quarrel. The smaller crossbow was the basic hand-missile weapon of besiegers and besieged throughout the Middle Ages. Used but apparently not appreciated by the Romans, the crossbow mysteriously disappeared for several centuries before its reintroduction into Europe, probably in eleventh-century Italy. In the First Crusade it proved a novelty to both Turks and Byzantine Greeks. Apparently a new, stronger trigger mechanism was responsible for the crossbow's resurgence. In the form best known in the twelfth and thirteenth centuries, it was cocked by means of a stirrup at the end of the stock, or crosspiece. Placing the weapon bow down, so that the stock was in a vertical position, the archer engaged the stirrup with his foot while hooking the bowstring to his belt.

He pushed down with his foot to cock the bow, which was caught and held by a trigger mechanism. Unhooking the string from his belt, the archer raised the weapon and fired by squeezing a lever under the stock. A range of up to 400 yards was attainable. The crossbow was exceptionally well suited to castle defense, for which the Welsh-English longbow, effective on the open battlefield, was less successful. The longbow had a shorter range and shot a lighter missile, and its greater portability and rapid rate of fire were of less account in castle defense than on the battlefield.

The chronicle *Annals of Dunstable* gave a vivid description of the capture of Bedford Castle, seat of the unruly lord Falkes de Bréauté, by the forces of Henry III in 1224, in an arduous eight-week siege. Falkes' castle consisted principally of two stone towers, an old and a new, separated by an inner bailey and surrounded by a broad outer bailey with a gate defended by a strong barbican.

> On the eastern side was a stone-throwing machine and two mangonels which attacked the [new] tower every day. On the western side were two mangonels which reduced the old tower. A mangonel on the south and one on the north made two breaches in the walls nearest them. Besides these, there were two wooden machines erected . . . overlooking the top of the tower and the castle for the use of the crossbowmen and scouts.
>
> In addition there were very many engines there in which lay hidden both crossbowmen and slingers. Further, there was an engine called a cat, protected by which underground diggers called miners . . . undermined the walls of the tower and castle.
>
> Now the castle was taken by four assaults. In the first the barbican was taken, where four or five of the outer guard were killed. In the second the outer bailey was taken, where more were killed, and in this place our people captured horses and their harness, corselets, crossbows, oxen, bacon, live pigs and other things beyond number. But the buildings with grain and hay in them they burned. In the third assault,

thanks to the action of the miners, the wall fell near the old tower, where our men got in through the rubble and amid great danger occupied the inner bailey. Thus employed, many of our men perished, and ten of our men who tried to enter the tower were shut in and held there by their enemies. At the fourth assault, on the vigil of the Assumption, about vespers, a fire was set under the tower by the miners so that smoke broke through into the room of the tower where the enemy were; and the tower split so that cracks appeared. Then the enemy, despairing of their safety, allowed Falkes' wife and all the women with her, and Henry [de Braybroke], the king's justice [whose capture by Falkes' brother William had caused the siege], with other knights whom they had shut up before, to go out unharmed, and they yielded to the king's command, hoisting the royal flag to the top of the tower. Thus they remained, under the king's custody, on the tower for that night.

On the following morning they were brought before the king's tribunal, and when they had been absolved from their excommunication by the bishops, by the command of the king and his justice they were hanged, eighty and more of them, on the gallows.

At the prayers of the leaders the king spared three Templars, so that they might serve Our Lord in the Holy Land in their habit. The chaplain of the castle was set free by the archbishop for trial in an ecclesiastical court . . . .

Falkes himself took the cross and was allowed to leave the country and go to Rome. The castle was dismantled except for the inner bailey, where living quarters were left for the Beauchamp family, earls of Bedford; the stones of the towers and outer bailey were given to local churches (poetic justice, since they had been built with the stones of two churches pulled down for that purpose by Falkes).

Garrisons surrendering at discretion were not usually so harshly dealt with. In ordinary conflict, without the added passion of religious difference or rebellion against authority, the whole garrison might be spared. Or the knights might be ransomed and the foot-soldiers massacred or mutilated. Often a rebel castle surrendered before it was absolutely necessary, in return for the garrison's being allowed to depart in freedom.

Even a castle sited on rock, well-provisioned with food and water, and stout-walled against artillery might still be taken by ruse. Usually the ruse was of the Trojan horse variety, that is, designed to effect entry by a small party. A popular trick was the nocturnal "escalade," a silent scaling of the wall at an inadequately guarded point. Another was a diversion designed to draw defenders away from a secondary gate or weak point that might then be suddenly overwhelmed. A third was penetration by means of a special ingress, such as a mine, a disused well, or a latrine, as in the case of Richard the Lionhearted's Château Gaillard in 1204. Occasionally the garrison might be lured into a sortie, so that the attackers could penetrate the gates as the defenders fled back into the castle.

Another form of ruse involved disguise. The attacking army might raise the siege and ostentatiously march away, but remain just out of sight. Some of its soldiers, donning the dress of peasants or merchants, might then gain access to the provision-hungry castle and seize the gatehouse. Knights were sometimes smuggled into a castle concealed in wagonloads of grain. The men of Count Baldwin of Flanders rescued their lord from imprisonment in a Turkish castle in 1123 by disguising themselves as peddlers and daggering the gate guards.

The dominant role of the siege helps explain one of the most characteristic aspects of medieval warfare: its stop-and-go, on-again-off-again pattern. Truces were natural between adversaries who might for long periods remain within ready range of communication but safe from each other's attack. In the war between Prince Louis of France and Henry III, at least five truces were made between

Château Gaillard: The keep of Richard the Lionhearted's stronghold on the Seine can be seen above the corrugated wall of the inner bailey. (Archives Photographiques)

October 1216 and February 1217, all related to castle sieges.

A shrewd commander besieging a castle might take advantage of a truce to plant a spy or bribe a member of the garrison. He might obtain valuable information, for example on the castle's supplies, or he might arrange for a postern to be opened at midnight or a rampart to be left unguarded. In 1265, a spy, apparently disguised as a woman, reported to Henry III's son Edward (later Edward I) that the garrison of Simon de Montfort's Kenilworth Castle planned to leave the stronghold for the night in order to enjoy baths in the town. According to the *Chronicle of Melrose*, the king's men surprised Simon's knights asleep and unarmed, and "some of them might be seen running off entirely naked, others wearing nothing but a pair of breeches, and others in shirts and breeches only."

Simon's son (Simon de Montfort III), in command of the party, regained the castle by swimming the Mere, the castle's lake, in his nightshirt. His father was killed three days later in the battle of Evesham, and the following spring young Simon had to defend Kenilworth Castle against the royal army. Despite a terrific pounding by siege engines, the castle held out against every assault, beating off a giant cat carrying 200 bowmen, and destroying another with a well-directed mangonel shot. Even the intervention of the archbishop of Canterbury had no effect; when the prelate appeared outside the castle to pronounce excommunication of the garrison, a defender donned clerical robes and jeered from atop the curtain wall. The king offered lenient terms, but Simon turned them down. It was nearly Christmas when Simon, his provisions exhausted, slipped out of the castle with his brothers to escape abroad, permitting his starving and dysentery-ridden garrison to surrender.

Bohemund d'Hauteville captured the powerful Saracen stronghold of Antioch by a combined bribe and ruse. Corrupting Firuz, an emir who commanded three towers, with promises of wealth, honor, and baptism, he had his own Frankish army feign withdrawal. That night the Franks returned stealthily and a picked band scaled the walls of Firuz' sector, killed resisting guards, and opened the gate. By morning the city was in the hands of Bohemund, who true to knightly tradition, even in a Crusade, had already extracted a promise from his fellow barons that the whole place would be turned over to him.

The chronicler of the *Gesta Stephani* related with relish the story of a ruse that was worked on Robert Fitz Hubert, one of the barons who rebelled against King Stephen and "a man unequaled in wickedness and crime," at least according to the partisan historian. Fitz Hubert took Stephen's Devizes Castle by a night escalade and then refused to turn it over to the earl of Gloucester, on whose side in the civil war he was supposed to be fighting. But Fitz Hubert came a cropper in negotiating with a neighbor baron, none other than John Fitz Gilbert the Marshal, father of William Marshal, whom the chronicler describes as "a man equally cunning and very ready to set great designs on foot by treachery." John had seized Marlborough, a strong castle belonging to the king. Fitz Hubert sent word to John that he would make a pact of peace and friendship, and that he wanted to parley with him at Marlborough. John agreed, but after admitting him to the castle behaved characteristically; he shut the gates behind him, "put him in a narrow dungeon to suffer hunger and tortures," then handed him over to the earl of Gloucester, who took him back to his own castle of Devizes and hanged him in sight of the garrison. The knights of the garrison then accepted a bribe and turned over the castle to the earl of Gloucester.

The following year, 1141, King Stephen's side scored a decisive victory in the war by another extraordinary military tactic, a siege of the besiegers. The Empress Matilda, Stephen's rival for the throne, and her brother, the earl of Gloucester, laid siege to the castle of the bishop of Winchester. The bishop appealed for help to Stephen's supporters—Stephen being at the moment a prisoner—and hired knights himself. Stephen's queen (also named Matilda) brought an army reinforced by troops nearly a thousand strong sent by the city of London. The besieged occupiers of the bishop's castle flung out firebrands, burning down the greater part of the town, including two abbeys, while Stephen's forces guarded the roads into the town to prevent provisions being brought to the townspeople, who were soon suffering from famine. By way of diversion, the earl of Gloucester began to fortify the abbey of Wherwell, six miles distant.

> But the king's forces . . . suddenly and unexpectedly arrived at Wherwell in an irresistible host, and attacking them

vigorously on every side they captured and killed a great
many, and at length compelled the rest to give way and take
refuge in the church. And when they used the church for
defense like a castle, the other side threw in torches from
every quarter and made them leave the church . . . . It was
indeed a dreadful and wretched sight, how impiously and
savagely bodies of armed men were ranging about in a
church, a house of religion and prayer, especially as in one
place mutual slaughter was going on, in another prisoners
were being dragged off bound with thongs, here the confla-
gration was fearfully ravaging the roofs of the church and the
houses, there cries and shrieks rang piercingly out from the
virgins dedicated to God who had left their cloisters with
reluctance under the stress of the fire.

The Empress Matilda and the earl of Gloucester decided
to raise the siege and save their army, but as the besiegers
were moving out of Winchester, the alert royal army fell
upon it from both sides and routed it. The chronicler
reports:

You could have seen chargers finely shaped and goodly to
look upon here straying about after throwing their riders,
there fainting from weariness and at their last gasp; shields
and coats of mail and arms of every kind lying everywhere
strewn on the ground; tempting cloaks and vessels of precious
metal, with other valuables, flung in heaps, offering themselves to the finders on every side.

Thus the defensive strength of a castle permitted an
offensive counterstroke to be launched. Sometimes a castle's
siege was tied into an even more complex strategic pattern.
In 1203 one of the few successes of King John in his war
against Philip Augustus involved such a pattern. The
French king was besieging the great castle of Arques,
southeast of Dieppe, held by John's garrison, while Philip's
ally, Arthur of Brittany, besieged Mirabeau, defended by a
force under his own grandmother, John's mother, Eleanor
of Aquitaine. William Marshal and two other Anglo-Nor-

Battle scene from the thirteenth-century Maciejowski Bible. Note escalade on the right; above the ladder a soldier, with an arrow through his body, flings a missile down from a tower; below, near the center of the picture, a crossbowman is about to fire at his companion, who wields a battle-axe against the climbing attacker. (Pierpont Morgan Library. MS. 638, f. 10v)

man earls were striving to relieve Arques when John struck a successful surprise blow at Arthur's army outside Mirabeau. Arthur's defeat exposed Philip to a combined attack by the armies of King John and William Marshal, compelling Philip to raise the siege of Arques without an arrow being fired. In retreat, Philip aimed a blow at William's small force, but William outdistanced him and escaped to Rouen. The following year John's inability to divert Philip from the long siege of the Château Gaillard brought the fall of that powerful castle, laying open the Seine valley to Philip and eventually leading to the surrender of Rouen and all Normandy.

Some castles underwent many sieges, others few, and some, like Chepstow, none. Unscathed Chepstow's history

Ruins of keep at Arques, Normandy, built by Henry I of England about 1125 and besieged by Philip Augustus in 1203. (Archives Photographiques)

underlines the castle's other military function, as a springboard for offensive action. Chepstow was deliberately designed as a base for aggression in Wales, and was put to effective use for this purpose by William Fitz Osbern and his Clare successors. On occasion Chepstow also served as a base for operations against the royal power, as in 1074, when William Fitz Osbern's son Roger and the earl of Norfolk rebelled against the Conqueror.

Pembroke Castle, on the southwest tip of Wales, provides an even more striking example than Chepstow of the aggressive role of the castle. In 1093, during the reign of William Rufus, Arnulph de Montgomery, a Norman baron, arrived at Pembroke by water, built a motte-and-bailey castle on a rocky peninsula on the site of an old Roman camp, and set about subduing the countryside. When Arnulph rebelled against Henry I in 1102, the king seized Pembroke Castle; in 1138 King Stephen granted it to Gilbert Strongbow de Clare, who fortified it; Gilbert's son Richard Strongbow used it as a base for the conquest of Ireland. Later William Marshal further strengthened the castle by building the great keep and hall. His son William Marshal II, reversing the procedure of Strongbow, brought a force from Ireland, where he served as justiciar, and employed Pembroke as a base for crushing the rebellious Welsh.

It was often the offensive capabilities of the castle that provoked sieges, but it was its incomparable defensive strength that conferred its military importance. Always ready, requiring little maintenance and repair, demanding scant advance notice of impending attack, the castle remained the basic center of power throughout the Middle Ages.

XI

The Castle Year

FOR THOSE WHO LIVED IN AND AROUND the medieval castle, the seasons of the year were marked by a succession of feast days consecrated by the Church but with pagan origins reaching far back in time. Four seasons, somewhat differently distributed from those of the modern calendar, were marked by ancient agricultural festivals in Christian guise.

Winter was the season from Michaelmas (September 29) to Christmas when wheat and rye were sown. From the end of the Christmas holidays to Easter was the season when spring crops were sown: oats, peas, beans, barley, and vetches. From the end of Easter week to Lammas (August 1) was summer, and from Lammas to Michaelmas was harvest, or autumn.

Christmas and Easter were the most important of the season-marking holidays, while Pentecost or Whitsunday, in Maytime (the seventh Sunday after Easter), was of almost equal moment. Each of these three great festivals was celebrated by a feast of the Church followed by a week or more of vacation, followed by another feast, not of the Church but of the people, to mark the resumption of work. Lesser religious holidays had unmistakable roots in husbandry: Candlemas (February 2), when tillage was resumed; Hocktide, at the end of Easter week, the beginning of summer; the three smaller Maytime feasts, Mayday, the Rogation Days, and Ascension; Midsummer, or St. John's Day, June 24; Lammas, the feast of St. Peter ad Vincula; and finally Michaelmas following the harvest.

Michaelmas marked not only the beginning of winter but the beginning of the castle's fiscal year. As the villagers opened the hedges to allow cattle to enter the harvested fields and graze on the stubble, and as plowing and harrowing began on the previously fallow fields, the castle stewards and manorial officers totaled up their accounts.

November was slaughter time, the "blood month" of the Anglo-Saxon calendar. Feed was too scarce to keep most of the animals through the winter, and smoked and salted meat was essential for human survival. The month began with the ancient feast of All Hallows, originally for the propitiation of evil spirits from the dead, but adapted by the Church as All Saints, followed next day by All Souls. Martinmas, or St. Martin's Day (November 11), marked another Christianized traditional holiday, the feast of the plowman—celebrated, at least in later days, with cakes, pasties, and *frumenty*, a pudding made of wheat boiled with milk, currants, raisins, and spices.

The dreary fortnight from Christmas Eve to Epiphany, or Twelfth Day (January 6), when the fields were drowned with rain or bound with frost, was transformed into the longest holiday of the year, a fourteen- or fifteen-day vacation. Services required of villeins were suspended, and the manorial servants—the hayward, the lord's plowman, the shepherd, swineherd, and oxherd—received their "per-

quisites," bonuses such as food, clothing, drink, and firewood, that were their traditional Christmas due.

Besides conviviality, carol singing, and entertainment,
the Christmas holidays brought a suspension of everyday
standards of behavior and status. On the eve of St. Nicholas'
Day (December 6), the cathedrals chose "boy bishops" who
presided over services on the Feast of the Holy Innocents
(December 28), assisted by schoolboys and choirboys. On
January 1, in the Feast of the Fools, priests and clerks wore
masks at mass, sang "wanton songs," censed with smoke
from the soles of old shoes, and ate sausages before the altar.
During the boisterous Christmas season the lord often
appointed a special force of watchmen for the twelve nights
in anticipation of rioting. Tenants on a manor belonging to
St. Paul's cathedral, London, were bound to watch at the
manor house from Christmas to Twelfth Day, their pay "a
good fire in the hall, one white loaf, one cooked dish, and a
gallon of ale [per day]."

During the Christmas season "every man's house, as also
their parish churches, was decked with holme [holly], ivy,
bay, and whatsoever the season of the year afforded to be
green," wrote William Fitzstephen in his description of
London in the twelfth century. On Christmas Eve the Yule
log was brought in—a giant section of tree trunk which
filled the hearth, and was kept burning throughout the
twelve nights.

Christmas brought celebration to the castle population
from bottom to top. Tenants on the manors owed special
rents but also enjoyed special privileges. Usually they owed
the lord bread, hens, and ale, which they brewed themselves, while in return he gave them Christmas dinner,
consisting mainly of the food they had provided; the lord
thus organized Christmas dinner at little cost to himself, the
tenants often even providing their own fuel, dishes, and
napkins. A group of three prosperous villeins on a manor

A puppet show. (Bodleian Library. MS. Bod. 264, f. 54v)

belonging to Wells Cathedral in the early fourteenth
century received "two white loaves, as much beer as they
will drink in the day, a mess of beef and of bacon with
mustard, one of browis [stew] of hen, and a cheese, fuel to
cook their food . . . and to burn from dinner time till even
and afterwards, and two candles." Another villein who held
less land was to have Christmas dinner, "but he must bring
with him . . . his own cloth, cup and trencher, and take
away all that is left on his cloth, and he shall have for
himself and his neighbors one wastel [loaf] cut in three for
the ancient Christmas game to be played with the said
wastel." The "ancient Christmas game" may have been a
version of "king of the bean," in which a bean was hidden
in a cake or loaf, and the person who found it became king
of the feast. Many of the manors of Glastonbury Abbey
gave Christmas feasts in the manor hall to which the tenant
brought firewood and his own dish, mug, and napkin "if he
wanted to eat off a cloth." Bread, broth, and beer were
served, and two kinds of meat, and the villeins were entitled
to sit drinking after dinner in the manor hall.

At the upper end of the scale, baron and king entertained
their knights and household with a feast and with gifts of
"robes" (outfits comprising tunic, surcoat, and mantle) and

jewels. In 1251 Matthew Paris complained that Henry III not only economized on his Christmas expenditures but exacted gifts from his subjects:

> At this most celebrated feast, the king (being perhaps saving in his anxiety about his pilgrimage) did not distribute any festive dresses to his knights and his household, although all his ancestors had made a practice from times of old of giving away royal garments and costly jewels. The usual richness and hospitality of the royal table was also diminished; and he now, without shame, sought his lodgings and his meals with abbots, priors, clerks, and men of low degree, staying with them and asking for gifts. And those persons were not considered courteous who did not, besides affording hospitality and splendid entertainments to him and his household, honor him and the queen, Prince Edward and the courtiers, separately with great and noble presents; indeed, he did not blush to ask for them, not as a favor, but as though they were his due . . . . Nor did the courtiers and royal household appreciate any presents unless they were rich and expensive; such as handsome palfreys, gold or silver cups, necklaces with choice jewels, imperial girdles, or such-like things.

All over Europe the twelve days of Christmas brought the appearance of the mummers, bands of masked pantomimists who paraded the streets and visited houses to dance and dice. A fourteenth-century mummery in London for the entertainment of Prince Richard (later Richard II), son of Edward the Black Prince, was described by John Stow:

> In the night, one hundred and thirty citizens, disguised and well-horsed, in a mummery, with sounds of trumpets, sackbuts [medieval trombones], cornets, shalmes [reed pipes], and other minstrels and innumerable torchlights of wax, rode to Kennington, near Lambeth, where the young Prince remained with his mother. In the first rank did ride forty-eight in likeness and habit of squires, two and two together, clothed in red coats and gowns of sendai [silk], with comely visors [masks] on their faces. After them came

Woman dancer. (Trustees of the British Museum. MS. Harl. 4951, f. 300v)

forty-eight knights, in the same livery. Then followed one richly arrayed, like an emperor; and after him some distance, one stately attired, like a pope, whom followed twenty-four cardinals; and after them eight or ten with black visors, not amiable, as if they had been legates from some foreign princes.

These maskers after they had entered the manor of Kennington alighted from their horses and entered the hall on foot; which done, the Prince, his mother, and the lords came out of the chamber into the hall, whom the mummers did salute, showing, by a pair of dice upon the table, their desire to play with the young Prince, which they so handled that the Prince did always win when he cast them . . . . After which they were feasted and the music sounded, the Prince and lords danced on the one part with the mummers, who did also dance; which jollity being ended, they were again made to drink, and then departed in order as they came.

In England, plays accompanied the mumming. The earliest of these "mummers' plays" now extant apparently date to the sixteenth century, but undoubtedly they had medieval ancestors. Mummers' plays appeared in many variations, and sometimes included a sword dance or a St.-George-and-the-dragon play, but always had a common theme, probably with a ritual origin, symbolizing the death and coming to life of all growing things: a fight in which a champion was killed and brought back to life when a doctor gave him a magic pill. Stock characters in the plays were a fool and a man dressed as a woman.

New Year's, like Christmas, was an occasion for gift giving, and Matthew Paris noted that in 1249 Henry III exacted from London citizens "one by one, the first gifts, which the people are accustomed superstitiously to call New Year's gifts." "First gifts" were omens of success for the coming year. So was the first person who entered the house after midnight, the "first-foot," who determined the fortunes of the family for the year. In some places this portentous visitor had to be a dark-complexioned man or boy, in others light-haired, while elsewhere it was considered desirable for him to be flat-footed.

On the manors, the resumption of work after the Christmas holidays was marked with special ceremonies honoring the plow and the "rock," the distaff. A feature of Plow Monday, the first Monday after Epiphany, was a plow race, beginning at sunrise, among the freemen of the village, who plowed part of the common pasture which was to be cultivated for the coming year, with each man trying to draw a furrow in as many different strips as he could; the ridges that he marked he could sow that year. A custom of later times that probably dated from even before the Middle Ages was that of the "fool-plow," hauled through the village by a group of young plowmen who asked for pennies from door to door. If anyone refused, they plowed up the ground before his door. Their leader was dressed as an old woman called Bessy, with a bullock's tail under his gown; sometimes they were accompanied by a man wearing a fox's skin as a hood and by a fool with a stick and bladder.

Little real plowing was done until Candlemas (February 2), a holiday formally known as the Feast of the Purification of the Virgin. It commemorated Mary's "churching," the ceremony of purification after childbirth in which the new mother donned her wedding gown and entered the church carrying a lighted candle. The village celebrated with a procession carrying candles. Candlemas was followed by Shrove Tuesday, a profane holiday dedicated to games and sports.

Throughout Lent the sanctuaries of the castle chapel as well as of the parish church were hung with veils, the cross and images shrouded. On Palm Sunday the parishioners carried yew or willow twigs in procession, following the Host and the Cross around the churchyard. On Good Friday the Cross was unveiled and set on the steps of the altar, the congregation coming forward to kiss it, kneeling and bowing low—"creeping to the Cross." Then the Cross and Host were buried in a special "Easter sepulchre" in the walls of the church or in a chapel, surrounded with candles. On Easter Eve all the fires and candles were extinguished, a new fire ceremonially kindled, and the great Paschal candle lit during an all-night vigil in the church. On Easter morning the sepulchre was opened and the Cross and Host carried to the altar.

Easter, like Christmas, was a day of exchanges between lord and tenant. Tenants brought the lord eggs; the lord gave his manorial servants dinner. The week that followed was a holiday for the villeins, celebrated with games; Fitzstephen described tilting at the quintain in boats on the Thames in London in the twelfth century during Easter week, while "Upon the bridge, wharfs and houses by the river side stand great numbers to see and laugh thereat."

Easter week ended with Hocktide, the second Monday and Tuesday after Easter, a two-day festival which in some places involved a custom of wives whipping husbands on Monday and husbands wives on Tuesday.

After Hocktide, medieval summer began with the Mayday celebrations, a time for lovemaking, when moral taboos were relaxed. Before daybreak the young people of the village and sometimes their elders, including even the clergy, joined in "bringing in the May," venturing into the woods to cut wildflowers, greenery, and hawthorn boughs. Sometimes they spent the night in the forest. The thirteenth-century romance *Guillaume de Dole* describes a Mayday celebration in Mainz, "a very gay city," in which the citizens passed the night in the woods "according to ancient custom," and in the morning "carried the May" through the city, singing, and hung it from windows and balconies. A young lord and lady of May were elected to preside over dances and games.

The Rogation Days, the Monday, Tuesday, and Wednesday before Ascension (the fortieth day after Easter), were celebrated in the countryside under the name of Gangdays. The people of the villages went "a-ganging" in a procession led by the priest and carrying the cross, banners, bells, and lights around the boundaries of the village, "beating its bounds" with willow wands. Small boys were ducked in brooks and ponds and their buttocks bumped against trees and rocks to help them memorize the village bounds. The procession halted at certain customary points, under a traditional oak or ash, while the priest said prayers and blessed the crops. Next came Whitsunday, the third and last of the Maytime feasts, with another week's holiday when villeins did not have to work for their lords.

In June, after sheep shearing, the feast of the summer solstice was celebrated: Midsummer, the eve of the Feast of the Nativity of St. John the Baptist (June 24). A thirteenth-century book of sermons describes St. John's Eve, when boys collected bones and rubbish and burned them, and carried brands about the fields, to drive away the dragons that were believed to be abroad poisoning the wells. A wheel was set afire and rolled down the hills, to signify that the sun had reached its highest point and was turning back.

St. John's Day was the traditional time to begin the hay harvest; Lammas (August 1) was the end of the harvest. Lammas—from the Anglo-Saxon *hlaf-mass* ("loaf mass")— was a feast of first fruits, a day when bread made from new wheat was blessed in church.

After Lammas came harvest time, the season when the villeins worked for the lord in the harvest boons, the *bidreaps.* On the last day of reaping, teams of workers raced each other to see which could first finish a ridge. Sometimes they left the last stand of corn for a ceremony, in which it was cut by the prettiest girl, or the reapers threw their sickles at it till it fell. The last sheaf might be decorated and brought in to the barn with music and merriment. In the evening the harvest-home supper was held, and in some places the villeins were bound to come to the lord's court to "sing harvest home"—to sing at the harvest feast.

With Michaelmas the cycle of the year began again.

One holiday varied locally: Wake Day. Most holidays were celebrated as wakes—eves—with people staying up late the night before the feast, always a treat for farmers as for children. But Wake Day, the feast of the parish saint, when congregations formed by separation from an older parish went in procession to honor the mother church, was an occasion for brawls and bloodshed, as parishes contended for precedence. In later times, and probably in the thirteenth century, people stayed up all night and in the morning went to a mass in honor of the patron saint, then spent the day in sports, usually in the churchyard. In the course of time some Wake Days became the occasion of important trade fairs.

Such was the course of the year for the thirteenth-century villager and for the castle-dweller whose existence depended on the village and its cycle of planting and harvesting.

A two-wheeled cart carries the shocks of grain to the barns. Luttrell Psalter. (Trustees of the British Museum. MS. Add. 42130, f. 175v) domini: a facie domini omnis terra.

Annunciauerunt celi iusticiam eius:
z uiderunt omnes populi gloriam
eius

Confundantur omnes qui ado
rant sculptilia: z qui gloriantur in
simulacris suis.

Adorate eum omnes angeli eius:
audiuit et letata est syon

Et exultauerunt filie iude: propter
iudicia tua domine

Quoniam tu dominus altissimus
super omnem terram: nimis exalta
tus es super omnes deos

XII

The Decline of the Castle

THE DECLINE IN MILITARY IMPORTANCE of the castle, apparent in the fourteenth century and rapidly accelerated in the fifteenth, is associated, like that of the armored knight, with the introduction of gunpowder. In the closing stage of the Hundred Years' War (1446–53), the old strongholds of western France that had withstood so many sieges fell with astonishing speed to the ponderous iron bombards, firing heavy stone cannonballs, of the French royal army. Yet the new weapons did not automatically and by themselves destroy the value of the castles. Thick masonry walls could stand even against cannonballs, and could furnish platforms for cannon of their own that would even enjoy certain advantages. Neither the castle nor the armored knight was automatically eliminated from war by the new firepower, and in fact both continued to take part in war throughout the sixteenth century and even later. At Chepstow in the seventeenth century, the battlements of some of the towers

Falaise, Normandy: Arrow loop in the curtain wall, showing modification for guns.

were modified for use with guns, and the southern curtain wall was thickened and its parapet loopholed for muskets. Bodiam Castle in Sussex, built in 1386 for coastal defense, had in its gatehouse gunports of keyhole design, of two sizes. In the sixteenth century Henry VIII built an array of castles along the southeast coast to carry cannon.

In the fifteenth-century War of the Roses in England, in the sixteenth-century religious wars in France, and in the seventeenth-century Civil War in England, body armor and castle walls played prominent but steadily diminishing roles. Their true destroyer was not gunpowder but central government. The rapid growth of major political units around monarchies (or dictatorships) was based to a great extent on the rapid growth of European cities with their wealthy merchant classes, whose money taxes provided the wherewithal to hire and supply large mercenary armies equipped with expensive cannon. A single knight might still be more effective on the battlefield than a foot soldier without armor and with a clumsy arquebus, but he was less valuable than ten such, and more expensive. The same sort of economics applied to castle building, with the added factor that the new political geography made obsolete many of the old frontier castles, such as those guarding the long-embattled English-Welsh and Norman-Breton-French borders.

Castles destroyed in the gunpowder era were usually razed rather than battle-damaged. Most of the English castles rallied to Charles I in the Civil War of the 1640s, and one after another were taken by the Puritans. Chepstow, never threatened in the Middle Ages, was breached and stormed; a plaque in the restored south curtain wall records the spot where its commandant, Sir Nicholas Kemeys, was killed. Even more seriously damaged by siege was Arundel, on whose barbican walls marks of cannonballs can still be seen, and much of whose extensive latter-day restoration was made necessary by its battering. More typical was the fate of Kenilworth, the rugged old stronghold of Simon de Montfort and his son that had fought the memorable siege of 1266. In 1649 a movement was begun in Parliament to demolish Kenilworth lest it become a center for renewed Royalist resistance, as had Pembroke, which

The castle of Angers, on the Maine near its juncture with the Loire: Southern gate of the great thirteenth-century curtain wall built by Louis IX. Note the thickened bases of the round towers and alternating courses of slate and limestone forming a striped pattern. The towers originally rose high above the curtain wall and were furnished with machicolations and conical pepper-pot roofs, but were decapitated during the religious wars of Henry III of France. (Archives Photographiques)

the year before had sustained a violent siege by Oliver Cromwell. Lord Monmouth, whose family had succeeded the Montforts as stewards of Kenilworth for the king, talked the government into merely "slighting" the castle—rendering it militarily useless by making gaps in the curtain and razing one wall of the keep.

A similar slighting of castles was carried out in France by Cardinal Richelieu at about the same time, usually by removing the heads of the towers. In obstinate cases, such as that of the youthful conspirator Cinq-Mars, Richelieu removed the head of the owner along with those of the towers of his castle on the Loire.

To the military obsolescence of the castle was added a domestic obsolescence. The desire for more comfortable and elegant living quarters, which had already modified the castle in the Middle Ages, by the seventeenth century had created a taste for purely residential palaces for the nobility. Sometimes an old castle or part of it was radically altered to turn it into a comfortable residence with light, heat, and other amenities, and it continued to be used, now and then, by the family that had originally built it. In other cases, ancient keeps were allowed to decay into picturesque ruins while next to them or in front of them elegant, many-windowed residences were built. In these new palaces the great hall, the basic living quarters of castles from the first motte-and-bailey strongholds to the domestic buildings of thirteenth-century castles, suffered a change. Expanded and elaborated throughout the Middle Ages, it now shrank and diminished in importance as the desire for privacy multiplied separate dining and "withdrawing" rooms for the castle family. The great hall of the thirteenth century finally dwindled into the servants' hall of the seventeenth.

Many castles no longer suitable for ordinary residential use found a more specialized purpose. Marten's Tower at Chepstow served as a comfortable prison for its single Puritan captive, but many others—the Tower of London,

Nogent-le-Retrou: Modern windows in the thirteenth-century gatehouse
of the Counts of Perche, southwest of Paris. To the left can be seen the
great rectangular keep, 110 feet high.

Paris' Bastille, and dozens more—provided grim quarters
for generations of prisoners, many political. Enlightenment
and prison reform at length did away with this inglorious
role, and some castles, especially those situated in capitals
and large towns, gained a more respectable one in conver-
sion to government archives, record centers, and bureaus.
Some, such as Gisors, in Normandy, furnished sites for
handsome public gardens. Many were converted to muse-

ums, notably Norwich Castle in England, which houses a fine collection of ancient and prehistoric British archaeological findings; Saumur, on the Loire, which contains both a decorative arts and a horse museum; and the Sforza Castle in Milan, with its rich archaeological and art galleries.

Yet amid such peaceful vocations, castles even in modern times occasionally reverted to their more heroic past. Some, such as Dover, continued to be garrisoned and armed in the nineteenth century and even the twentieth, and in both World Wars castles all over Europe saw combat duty. Many English coastal castles, including ancient Hastings, served as observation posts and antiaircraft-gun emplacements. In 1940 at Pevensey, built by the Normans within the walls of one of the third-century Roman forts of the "Saxon coast," two machine-gun posts and a pillbox were incorporated into the Roman walls, disguised as part of the original enceinte, in preparation against a German invasion. Four years later the ancient fort became a radio direction center for the U.S. Air Corps. In France, Germany, and Italy, castles repeatedly served as strong points and refuges against small-arms and even artillery fire. GIs of the U.S. 42nd Division, for example, found the walls of Wurzburg Castle, Germany, in 1945 very satisfactory protection against German 88-mm. projectiles from across the Main River, modern thin-shelled high explosives proving much less damaging to masonry than the stone cannonballs of the fifteenth-century bombards.

But the final role of the European medieval castle seems to be that of tourist attraction. In Britain, France, Germany, Spain, Italy, and elsewhere, with the aid of a guide or a guidebook and some imagination, one can stand in the grassy bailey and re-people the weathered stone ramparts and towers and the vanished wooden outbuildings with archers and knights, servants, horses, and wagoners, the lord and lady and their guests, falcons and hunting dogs, pigs and poultry—all the unkempt, unsafe, unsavory but irresistibly appealing life of the thirteenth century.

Glossary of Castle Terms

Allure	Wall-walk, passage behind the parapet of a castle wall
Bailey	Courtyard
Ballista	Engine resembling a crossbow, used in hurling missiles or large arrows
Barbican	An outwork or forward extension of a castle gateway
Buttery	Room for the service of beverages
Cat	Assault tower
Catapult	Stone-throwing engine, usually employing torsion
Chemise	Inner walled enclosure of a castle
Corbel	A stone or timber bracket supporting a projection from a wall
Crenelation	A notched battlement made up of alternate crenels (openings) and merlons (square saw-teeth)
Curtain	A castle wall enclosing a courtyard
Donjon or keep	The inner stronghold of a castle

Drawbridge	A wooden bridge leading to a gateway, capable of being raised or lowered
Enceinte	An enclosing wall, usually exterior, of a fortified place
Escalade	Scaling of a castle wall
Forebuilding	A projection in front of a keep or donjon, containing the stairs to the main entrance
Garderobe	Latrine
Hall	Principal living quarters of a medieval castle or house
Keep	See donjon
Machicolation	A projection in the battlements of a wall with openings through which missiles can be dropped on besiegers
Mangonel	A form of catapult
Merlon	Part of a battlement, the square "sawtooth" between crenels
Meurtrière	Arrow loop, slit in battlement or wall to permit firing of arrows, or for observation
Motte	An earthwork mound on which a castle was built
Oriel	Projecting room on an upper floor (in the medieval sense; later an upper-floor bay window)
Parapet	Protective wall at the top of a fortification, around the outer side of the wall-walk
Portcullis	Vertical sliding wooden grille shod with iron suspended in front of a gateway, let down to protect the gate
Postern or sally-port	Secondary gate or door
Ram	Battering-ram
Sapping	Undermining, as of a castle wall
Screens	Wooden partition at the kitchen end of a hall, protecting a passage leading to buttery, pantry, and kitchen
Solar	Originally a room above ground level, but commonly applied to the great chamber or a private sitting room off the great hall

Springald	War engine of the catapult type, employing tension
Trebuchet	War engine developed in the Middle Ages employing counterpoise
Ward	Courtyard or bailey

Glossary of Feudal Terms

Aid	A special obligation of a vassal to provide money for such occasions as his lord's ransom, the marriage of his daughter, the knighting of his son, or for going on Crusade
Almoner	Official appointed to distribute alms
Bailiff	Manorial official, overseer of the manor, chosen by the lord
Baron	Noble of high rank, in England a tenant-in-chief holding his lands directly from the king
Benefice	The grant made by a lord, usually of land
Castle-guard	Feudal obligation to serve in the garrison of a castle, either for a period each year or during war
Castellan	Governor of a castle
Chamberlain	Household official in charge of the lord's chamber
Chaplain or chancellor	Priest or monk in charge of the chapel and of the secretarial department of the castle

Chevauchée
(cavalcade)   Feudal duty to accompany the lord on a minor expedition or as an escort

Colée or buffet   Traditional blow administered to the newly made knight at his dubbing

Curia Regis   English royal council and court of justice

Demesne   Land held directly by its owner

Earl   Count; highest English title in the Middle Ages

Eyre   English circuit court

Fief, fee, or feud Land or revenue-producing property granted by a lord in return for a vassal's service

Frankpledge   Medieval English police measure by which a community was divided into groups or tithings, each group responsible for the conduct of its members and for producing them in court if they committed a breach of the law

Hallmote   Manorial court

Hayward   Manorial official in charge of the *haies*, or hedges

Heriot   A death-duty to the lord; in the case of a villein on a manor, usually the best beast

Honor   Great estate of a tenant-in-chief

Host or ost   Feudal military service in the lord's army

Justiciar   Regent in England under William I, chief minister until the 1220s

Manor   Estate held by a lord and farmed by tenants who owed him rents and services, and whose relations with him were governed by his manorial court

Marcher lord   Lord of a border district, such as the boundaries of Wales and Scotland

Marshal   Household official in charge of the stables, later a royal officer

Mesnie   Military personnel of a castle household

Quintain   Dummy with shield mounted on a post, used as a target in tilting

Provost   Feudal or royal magistrate

Reeve	Manorial overseer, usually a villager elected by tenants of the manor
Regalian	Royal
Relief	A fine paid by the heir of a vassal to the lord for the privilege of succeeding to an estate
Scutage	Shield-tax, a tax paid in lieu of military service
Seneschal or steward	Manager of an estate or a household
Sheriff	Royal official in charge of a shire or county
Squire	Knight-aspirant
Vassal	A person granted the use of land in return for homage, fealty, and military service
Villein	A non-free man, owing heavy labor service to a lord, subject to his manorial court, bound to the land, and subject to certain feudal dues
Woodward	A private forester

Great Medieval Castles: A Geographical Guide

A CATALOG OF EVEN THE MOST IMPORTANT and interesting medieval castles could occupy a volume, and the following list is only a sampling. The many post-medieval castles whose battlements served purely decorative purposes long after military and economic history made them otherwise obsolete are excluded. Even nineteenth-century America built such replicas, in a profusion that justified a recent book on "American castles." Those below all belong to the Middle Ages. Within each region they are listed chronologically, in accordance with the local historical development of the castle.

ENGLAND

English medieval castles embrace the whole history of castle-building, from the eleventh-century motte-and-bailey (of which many earthwork traces remain, some crowned by later shell keeps) to the mighty Edwardian fortresses of the late thirteenth and early fourteenth centuries, whose formidable curtain walls, gatehouses, and towers, built on carefully chosen sites, represent the ultimate in medieval defensive works.

Berkhamsted.   25 miles northwest of London. One of the earliest Anglo-Norman castles, with both motte and bailey surrounded by wet moats; the ruins of a shell keep; thirteenth-century outworks.

Warwick.   75 miles northwest of London. A motte-and-bailey fortified by William the Conqueror in 1068, converted to a shell keep late in the eleventh century, with fourteenth- and fifteenth-century walls and towers and residential buildings of the seventeenth century.

York.   80 miles north of London. Two motte-and-bailey castles, built in 1068 and 1069, the former now surmounted by Clifford's Tower (1245).

Windsor.   20 miles west of London. The Round Tower, shell wall built about 1170 on a motte constructed in 1070, previously guarded by a wooden tower; curtain walls built by Henry II late in the twelfth century and by Henry III in the thirteenth; chapel and residential buildings by later kings.

Launceston.   Cornwall. Stone shell wall added in the twelfth century to motte of 1080; round inner tower built in the thirteenth century.

Totnes.   Devon. Motte of 1080 enclosed by a late twelfth century shell wall; hall built in the bailey below in the thirteenth century; shell wall rebuilt early in the fourteenth century.

Restormel.   Cornwall. Twelfth-century shell wall with projecting square tower; domestic quarters, barracks and chapel added in the thirteenth century around the inside of the wall with a central court.

White Tower (Tower of London).   Rectangular keep built in 1080, 90 feet high to the battlements, originally of three stories, divided internally by a cross-wall; the topmost story, with the great hall, solar, and chapel, rises the height of two floors; entrance was by a forebuilding, now destroyed; the towers of the inner curtain and parts of the walls themselves date from the late twelfth and the thirteenth centuries, such as the Wakefield Tower, where the Crown Jewels are kept, and the Bloody Tower, where the little princes Edward V and his younger brother Richard are believed to have been murdered on the instructions of Richard III, and where Sir Walter Raleigh was imprisoned. Both towers were built in the reign of Henry III.

Colchester.   50 miles northeast of London. Rectangular keep built in 1087, with three stories.

Rochester.   25 miles east of London. Great keep with a parapet 113 feet high and corner towers rising 12 feet higher, built in 1130, with three residential floors above a basement; the entire building is divided internally from top to bottom by a cross-wall; entrance is in a forebuilding.

Dover.   Rectangular keep built in the 1180s by Henry II, 83 feet high, with turrets at the corners 12 feet higher, three stories, entrance to the main (third) floor in a forebuilding that also contains two chapels; keep divided internally by a cross-wall into two large halls in each story, with chambers in the walls; curtain walls of the thirteenth century.

Kenilworth.   80 miles northwest of London. Rectangular keep called Caesar's Tower, built 1150–75, of exceptionally powerful construction, walls 14 feet thick, strengthened by buttresses and massive corner turrets; two stories, one large hall in each story, original entrance to the second story by external stairs; curtain walls of the thirteenth century; great hall built by John of Gaunt in the fourteenth century.

Orford.   75 miles northeast of London on the Suffolk coast. Built 1166–70, circular internally, multiangular externally, with three large square turrets; three stories, hall on the second floor, forebuilding containing entrance porch at the second-story level, with chapel above; spiral stairway to the basement and battlements in one turret, chambers in the other turrets.

Conisborough. 145 miles north of London. Built 1180–90, tall cylindrical tower with very thick walls supported by six massive buttresses the height of the building, commanding the whole front of the keep; vaulted basement, three upper floors, original entrance at the second story reached by a drawbridge; sloping base to prevent attackers from approaching close to the keep.

Pembroke. Wales. Round keep built about 1190, 54 feet in diameter, 80 feet high, with four stories; the entrance to the second story is by stairs in a forebuilding leading to a drawbridge before the doorway; a spiral stairway from the entrance floor leads to the basement and the upper floors and battlements; halls and living rooms are in the inner bailey near the keep.

Edwardian Castles of Wales. Most of them are in a good state of preservation: Beaumaris, Caernarvon, Caerphilly, Conway, Denbigh, Flint, Harlech, Kidwelly, Rhuddlan.

France

Like England, France has extant castles representing all the architectural types.

Langeais. On the Loire. Rectangular keep built by Fulk Nerra about 1010, with three stories: first and second floors for storage, hall on the third story; the rest of the present castle was built by Louis XI in the fifteenth century.

Loches. On the Indre, south of the Loire. Four-story rectangular keep built about 1020, 122 feet high, with a large forebuilding; thirteenth-century curtain walls, fifteenth-century Round Tower and square Martelet Tower.

Gisors. Normandy. Shell keep built early in the twelfth century, four-story tower with irregular octagonal plan added by

Henry II of England on the motte late in the century; Tour du Prisonnier added in 1206—a round keep incorporated in the curtain wall, with three vaulted stories entered at third-story level from a wall-walk on the curtain on one side, a postern at the same level on the other side, stairways to lower floors from the third story, the tower a self-contained residence.

Arques.   Near Dieppe. Great rectangular keep built by Henry I of England about 1125, with four stories; entrance on the third story by a stairway built around two sides of the keep and protected by an outer wall; partition wall dividing the lower three floors each into two large halls with no communication between them except by a complicated system of wall passages and stairways; top floor command-post undivided. The castle is now known as Arques-la-Bataille because of Henry IV's victory there in 1589 in the French civil war.

Houdan.   30 miles west of Paris. Built about 1130, square on the inside, circular on the outside, with four projecting semicircular turrets; two very high stories, ground floor storeroom, second-story hall with chambers in three of the turrets, spiral stairs in the fourth leading to battlements and basement, original entrance in this turret twenty feet above ground reached by a drawbridge from a wall-walk on the curtain wall of the castle, now destroyed.

Étampes.   30 miles south of Paris. Built about 1160, large four-lobed three-story keep built around a central pier, vaulted great hall on the second story, chambers on the third story, entrance midway between floors, probably reached by a wall-walk and drawbridge from the curtain, now destroyed.

Châteaudun.   70 miles southwest of Paris on the Loir River. Round keep built early in the twelfth century, one of the earliest and best preserved of its type; 95 feet high, containing three floors, the lower two covered with domes; entrance on the second floor; chapel and block of residential buildings built by Joan of Arc's companion-at-arms, Dunois.

La Roche Guyon.   On the Seine 35 miles northwest of Paris. Round keep built in the last half of the twelfth century on a precipitous cliff, with ascent from the riverbank by subterranean stairways and narrow ledges cut through the rock; a central tower is surrounded by a chemise and an outer wall, and all three are prow-shaped, the prow pointing away from the cliff and toward the line of approach from above.

Château Gaillard. Normandy. Built by Richard the Lion-hearted in 1198 on a precipitous cliff 300 feet above the Seine, with three baileys arranged in line; the keep, in the inner bailey, on the edge of the precipice, is circular and thickened by a prow at the side toward the bailey; the keep was once protected by machicolations (now destroyed), one of the earliest examples of stone machicolations in Western Europe; the great hall is near the keep in the inner bailey; the curtain of the inner bailey is protected by corrugations on its outer face rather than by wall towers; the curtains of the outer and middle baileys are strengthened by circular wall towers.

Chinon. On the Vienne. Three groups of buildings: the Fort St. Georges, where Henry II of England died in 1189; the Château du Milieu, where Joan of Arc met the Dauphin in 1429; and the Château du Coudray, with its Tour du Coudray, built by Philip Augustus early in the thirteenth century, a round keep with stairways along the inside of the walls, guarded at each turn by machicolations, leading to the upper stories. The Templars were held for trial in the Tour du Coudray in 1308.

Angers. On the Maine near its juncture with the Loire, on the site of an earlier castle built by Fulk Nerra of Anjou. Great curtain wall built by Louis IX, 1230–40, with seventeen round towers with thickened bases rising almost half the height of the towers, two posterns, a chapel and residential quarters, no keep.

Tour de Constance. Aigues-Mortes, Provence. Built in the mid-thirteenth century, a large circular keep isolated by a moat at one corner of the city's fortifications, originally a castle in itself before the town walls were built; two vaulted stories with large halls over a small basement.

Fougères.   Brittany. Represents many periods of castle building, from the foundations of a round keep razed by Henry II of England in 1166 to the thirteenth-century curtain walls, the Melusine and Gobelin Towers of the thirteenth and fourteenth centuries, and the fifteenth-century Surienne and Raoul Towers; the stone columns that supported the second story of the great hall can still be seen in the inner bailey; entrance to the castle is protected by a moat, a barbican, and four towers. Fougères is unusual in that it is built on a plain, with the neighboring town on a hilltop.

Najac.   Southern France. Built 1250–60, a three-story vaulted round keep consisting of one of the corner towers of a rectangular curtain wall equipped with an elaborate system of stairways and passages; the entrance to the keep on the ground floor is protected by a moat and drawbridge, and a spiral stairway rises from the entrance to the upper floors and battlements; the great hall is on the second story; all operations were directed from the keep, and each section of the defensive system was capable of being isolated by barriers.

Vincennes.   On the eastern edge of Paris. Early fourteenth century, great 170-foot-high keep containing the king's living quarters, isolated from the rest of the castle by a chemise and a wide moat, and strongly fortified; a first-story basement and kitchen, royal apartments on the second and third stories; the fourth story occupied by attendants, the fifth by servants, the sixth used for defense.

Pierrefonds.   45 miles northeast of Paris. Built by Louis d'Orléans, count of Valois, 1390–1400, on a rocky height; strong double curtain walls, the inner defended by eight round towers; barracks and service quarters built around the inner courtyard; the count's residence in a tall keep near the gate, capable of independent defense; approach route between curtain walls around the whole enclosure, then through a barbican and across a drawbridge; restored in the nineteenth century by Viollet-le-Duc.

ITALY

Italian castles belong to four classes: Dark Age castles; Norman fortresses built after the conquest of southern Italy beginning in the 1040s; castles built in the thirteenth century by Frederick II all over Italy and Sicily, sometimes on the foundations of Norman castles; and castles built by the despots in the fourteenth and fifteenth centuries, many of them in the cities.

Canossa. Emilia. Picturesque ruins of a tenth-century fortress perched on a rock, scene of the famous barefoot-in-the-snow penance of Emperor Henry IV in 1077 during the investiture controversy with Pope Gregory VII.

Bari. Southern Italy. Castle built by the Norman ruler of Sicily, Count Roger I, in 1131, and rebuilt in 1233 by Emperor Frederick II; corner towers and inner court added in the sixteenth century.

Barletta. Southern Italy. Eleventh-century Norman castle rebuilt by the Hohenstaufens, enlarged by Charles of Anjou late in the thirteenth century.

Capuan Castle. Naples. Built by the Normans in the eleventh century, remodeled by Emperor Frederick II in the thirteenth century.

Castel Nuovo. Naples. Built by the Angevins in 1282, modeled on the castle of Angers; five round towers added in the fifteenth century by Alfonso I of Aragon.

Castles of Frederick II. Characteristically, these have rectangular enclosures with square corner towers. *Lucera,* a great square tower with an enclosed court, and a curtain wall added late in the thirteenth century by Charles of Anjou; *Gioia del Colle,* Apulia; *Prato,* northwest of Florence; *Gravina,* Apulia, a hunting castle; *Castello Ursino,* Catania, a rectangular enclosure with round towers; *Castel del Monte,* Apulia, octagonal with eight octagonal towers and inner octagonal court.

Gradara. On the Adriatic coast south of Rimini. Square castle with round corner towers built in the thirteenth century by the Grifi family, afterward owned by the Malatestas and the Sforzas; here Giovanni Malatesta is supposed to have murdered his wife, Francesca da Rimini, and her lover, Paolo, in the tragic love story immortalized by Dante.

Castello di Sarzanello. North of Pisa. Built by the Luccan despot Castruccio Castracane in 1322; thick triangular curtain wall with round towers, surrounded by a deep moat, with a square keep commanding a bridge that links the enclosure to a detached bastion.

Scaliger Castle. Verona. Built by Can Grande II della Scala in 1354 on the Adige River, with the square tower of the keep guarding a fortified bridge.

Castello della Rocca. Cesena (near Rimini). Castle of the Malatestas, built about 1380, with a polygonal inner bailey on top of a hill and an outer bailey running down the slope; the inner bailey is surrounded by powerful walls with towers at the angles, and protected by a strongly defended gatehouse and a small barbican; the approach to the barbican is intercepted by cross-walls forming a winding passage with gateways at the turning points.

Castello d'Este. Ferrara. Built about 1385, on level ground, with a rectangular curtain that has square towers at each corner; guarded by moats and four gatehouses with drawbridges; living quarters are built around an internal courtyard.

Castello Visconteo. Pavia. Built by the Visconti family in the late fourteenth century, surrounded by walls nearly 100 feet high, punctuated by square corner towers.

Castello San Giorgio. Mantua. Built by the Gonzagas in the late fourteenth century; a square enclosure with powerful square corner towers and machicolations; surrounded by a deep moat.

Castello Sforzesco.   Milan. A huge square brick castle, the largest castle in Italy, built by Francesco Sforza in 1412 on the site of a Visconti fortress of 1368, with curtain walls 12 feet thick, a gatehouse, and two great round towers at the front corners; the interior is divided into one large and two small courtyards, and the smallest, the *rochetta,* which comprises the inner fortress, is guarded by a square tower with machicolations.

SPAIN

Spain, like Italy, has some of the oldest castles in Europe. Those of Spain fall into four categories: Muslim castles, before the twelfth century; castles of the Christian military orders, late twelfth and early thirteenth century; castles built during the Reconquest to protect important centers; and castle-palaces of the fifteenth century. The Muslim castles, which were later imitated by the Christian military orders, were typically built of *tapia,* a combination of pebbles and mortar, and were rectangular, with square wall towers and a square extramural tower; points in the curtain walls needing stronger defense were protected by pentagonal towers. Later Christian castles were often of brick.

Almeria.   Province of Granada, on the Mediterranean coast. Built by the Moors in the eighth century on the site of a Phoenician fortress; a great enclosure with square towers on top of a ridge; captured by the Christians in 1147, recaptured by the Muslims in 1157 and held by them until 1489; round towers added by Ferdinand and Isabella.

Baños de la Encina.   Near Jaén, south central Spain. Castle built by the Moors in 967 to defend the Guadalquivir River; rectangular enclosure with square towers on a hilltop; captured in 1212 by the Christians, who built an extramural tower for an added defense.

Alcala de Guadaira.   Province of Seville. Muslim castle, curtain walls with eight square towers, one defending the gate, and an extramural tower protecting the bridge leading to the gate; cross-walls dividing the attacking forces into separate sectors.

Gormaz.   Castile. Built by the Muslims in the tenth century on top of a limestone rock, given to the famous hero-adventurer, the Cid, at the end of the eleventh century by Alfonso VI; two baileys, irregular plan, with square towers, curtain wall 30 feet high and 3,000 feet long.

Almodovar del Rio.   Province of Cordoba. Muslim castle high on the banks of the Guadalquivir River, used as a treasure house in the fourteenth century by Peter the Cruel; has high, crenelated walls; an extramural tower 130 feet high is connected to the rest of the castle by a high stone bridge.

Calatrava la Nueva.   Castile. Built by the military Order of Calatrava about 1216 on the site of an Arab castle; the main enclosure has an irregular octagonal shape and is surrounded by a moat; there is a second enclosure to protect livestock, an extramural tower, a great church with a rose window.

Zorita de los Canes.   Province of Guadalajara. Castle originally built by the Muslims, conquered in 1085 by Alfonso VI, reconquered by the Arabs in the twelfth century, later taken over by the Order of Calatrava, who rebuilt it; on a mound overlooking the Tagus River; an outer curtain has powerful towers, the southern serving as a keep; an extramural tower on the northeast is connected to the castle by a solid Gothic arch; entrance to the castle is through an arched gateway protected by a gatehouse.

Consuegra.   Province of Toledo. Built by the Hospitallers in the twelfth century and modeled after the Crusader castles of Syria; double-walled enceinte, central keep with round towers.

La Mota.   Medina del Campo, north of Madrid. Built about 1440 on the ruins of a thirteenth-century castle; outer curtain wall with two galleries in its thickness, tall rectangular keep with four pairs of turrets at the corners, machicolations between; favorite residence of Columbus' patroness Isabella, who died here in 1504; later her daughter Joanna the Mad was imprisoned here, as was Cesare Borgia (who managed to escape).

Peñafiel. North of Madrid. Built about 1450, following the contours of the top of an eminence above the Duero River; a long narrow enclosure with two lines of curtain walls strengthened by round towers, a square central tower-keep 112 feet high.

Alcazar. Segovia. Built by Alfonso VI late in the eleventh century, rebuilt in the 1350s; on a rocky eminence; the walls are strengthened with semicircular towers; there are two great square towers within the enclosure.

Coca. Northwest of Madrid. A brick castle built by Muslim workmen for the archbishop of Seville, Alfonso de Fonseca, in the fifteenth century; massive square double curtain walls are surrounded by a moat; the keep is an enlarged square tower of the inner enclosure guarding the entrance; the crenelations are decorated with distinctive rounded furrows; there are embrasures for cannon, square cross-and-orb gun loops, hexagonal projecting turrets from corner towers of external wall.

Germany and Austria

An early German or Austrian castle was characterized by its inaccessible site, usually on top of a rocky height, and by its square central *Bergfried,* or tower; later many castles were built on level ground surrounded by moats. The greatest period of medieval castle-building in Germany was the era of the Hohenstaufens (1138–1254). Most of the famous "Castles on the Rhine" now exist either in ruins or in restorations.

Marksburg. On the Rhine. Built originally in the tenth century to collect tolls on the Rhine, enlarged in the thirteenth to fifteenth centuries, restored by Kaiser Wilhelm II; square central tower, residential quarters, series of gatehouses guarding approach to the upper castle.

Trifels. Rhenish Palatinate. Castle of the German emperors built in the eleventh century on top of a high eminence, expanded in the twelfth and thirteenth centuries by the Hohenstaufens; here Richard the Lionhearted was kept prisoner in 1193 by Emperor Henry VI; 70-foot-high rectangular keep, chapel; castle almost wholly reconstructed. Ruins of two other castles, *Anebos* and *Scharfenberg,* are on nearby peaks.

Munzenberg. Hesse. Built 1174; elliptical enclosure on top of a mountain, with two round towers and a forward tower guarding the west approach; living quarters, chapel and kitchen along the inside of the curtain.

Wildenberg. Bavaria. Late twelfth century, rectangular enclosure on top of a mountain; square towers guarding the line of approach.

Eltz. On the Moselle. Begun by the counts of Eltz in 1157, mostly dating from the thirteenth to the sixteenth centuries; the oldest surviving structure is the Platteltz Tower (twelfth or thirteenth century), partly restored after a fire in the 1920s; nearby are the ruins of *Trutzeltz,* the castle of the archbishop of Trier, who carried on a protracted feud with the counts of Eltz and finally compelled them to surrender.

Heidenreichstein. Austria. Built in the twelfth century; a square tower was added in the thirteenth century, a round tower later.

Rapottenstein. Austria. Built in the twelfth century on a rock outcropping; there are a round tower defending the approaches, a square tower higher up, and residential buildings.

Ortenberg. Bavaria. Early thirteenth century; three baileys, the inner and middle in a line, the outer bailey in front of both, with a rising approach; the enemy had to pass the length of the outer bailey under attack from the inner and middle ones, then up a flight of steps and through a barbican and three other gateways before the inner bailey was reached; a trapezoidal keep at the highest point is surrounded closely by the wall of the inner bailey.

Falkenberg. Bavaria. Built about 1290 on a huge natural pile of boulders overlooking the Waldnaab River; the curtain follows the contour of the rocks; the buildings of the castle are between the curtain and a small internal courtyard containing a square keep.

Hohensalzburg. Austria. Residence of the archbishop of Salzburg, built in the twelfth century on a rock 400 feet above the Salzach River; modeled after the Crusader castles, later enlarged and remodeled; massive curtain walls, round towers.

OTHER EUROPEAN CASTLES

Pfeffengen and *Dornach.* Switzerland. Two shell keeps of the twelfth and early thirteenth centuries built within a few miles of each other; in both cases, the shell wall, instead of being built on top of the mound, is built against its vertical sides, containing the mound and rising high above it.

Chillon. Switzerland. Castle made famous by Byron's poem; built in the thirteenth century on the site of a ninth-century castle, on a rocky island in a lake, reached by a bridge leading to a gatehouse; the curtain wall follows the contours of the rock, and the buildings of the castle are constructed around the inner court, with a square keep at the end farthest from the bridge.

Castle of the Counts of Flanders. Ghent. Built in 1180, on the site of an eleventh-century fortress, by Philip of Alsace on his return from Crusade, and modeled on the Crusader castles; on level ground, surrounded by a moat and high curtain walls with round towers; a rectangular keep has a lesser hall on the first floor, the great hall above.

Carrickfergus.   Northern Ireland. Built on the shores of Belfast Loch, c. 1180–1205; square Norman keep joined to curtain walls.

Trim.   Ireland. Built c. 1190–1200, the largest Anglo-Norman castle in Ireland; square keep with projecting wings, thirteenth-century curtain walls with round towers.

CRUSADER CASTLES

From a strictly military point of view, the castles built by the Templars, Hospitallers, and other Crusaders are incomparable. Drawing on European, Byzantine, and Muslim models and on their own experience, the Crusaders built strongholds of immense size and ingeniously related defenses in which small garrisons, supplied for as much as five years, could defy large armies.

Saone (Sahyun).   Syria. The best-preserved Crusader castle, with a half mile of fortification in the shape of a rough isosceles triangle atop a mountain spur, the two long sides fronting on precipitous cliffs, the base on a 60-foot-wide, 90-foot-deep moat hewn out of the rock, a "needle" of the rock left to act as a bridge pier, with a drawspan to the postern; the square keep built against the curtain wall on the moat side.

Krak des Chevaliers.   Syria. The giant "Citadel [*Krak*] of the Knights," the most powerful and famous of the Crusader castles, almost as well preserved as Saone; begun early in the twelfth century and strengthened by the Hospitallers in 1142; two concentric walls enclose two baileys, an outer and an inner, the latter high on the spur of Gebel Alawi. Besieged at least twelve times, this castle "stuck like a bone in the throat of the Saracens," in the words of a Muslim writer; in one siege, that of 1163, the Hospitallers not only held off the army of Nur-ed-Din but sallied out to surprise and defeat it; even in 1271, a lone outpost in a Muslim sea, its garrison down to 300 knights, the Krak held out until the Muslim general Baibars tricked the defenders with a forged order, after which he chivalrously gave the knights safe conduct to the coast.

Anamur.   A seacoast castle in Turkey, with a huge fourteen-sided tower dominating the beach, and three baileys, one facing the land, one the sea, and a third on high ground between the two.

Chastel Pélérin ("Pilgrim Castle").   Israel. Built by the Templars in 1218 and well supplied with artillery and heavily garrisoned when the Muslims besieged it unsuccessfully in 1220, it was never taken, but was abandoned in 1291 after the fall of nearby Acre, and afterward badly damaged by Muslim engineers quarrying it to rebuild the city.

Bibliography

CHAPTER I. *The Castle Comes to England*

ANDERSON, W. F. D., *Castles of Europe: from Charlemagne to the Renaissance*. London, 1970.

The Anglo-Saxon Chronicle, trans. James Ingram. London, 1923.

ARMITAGE, ELLA, *Early Norman Castles*. London, 1912.

BAYET, MARIE, *Les Châteaux de France*. Paris, 1927.

BEELER, JOHN, *Warfare in England, 1066–1189*. Ithaca, N.Y., 1966.

———, *Warfare in Feudal Europe, 730–1200*. Ithaca, N.Y., 1971.

BRAUN, HUGH, *The English Castle*. London, 1936.

BROOKE, CHRISTOPHER, *From Alfred to Henry III, 871–1272*. Edinburgh, 1961.

BROWN, R. ALLEN, *Dover Castle*. London, 1966 (Ministry of Works).

———, *Rochester Castle*. London, 1969 (Ministry of Works).

CLEATOR, P. E., *Castles and Kings*. London, 1963.

COTTRELL, LEONARD, *The Roman Forts of the Saxon Shore*. London, 1971 (Department of the Environment).

DAVIS, H. W. C., *England Under the Normans and Angevins, 1066–1272.* London, 1937.

DOUGLAS, DAVID C., *The Norman Achievement, 1050–1100.* Berkeley, 1969.

———, *William the Conqueror: the Norman Impact upon England.* Berkeley, 1967.

DUTTON, RALPH, *The Châteaux of France.* London, 1957.

ECHAGÜE, JOSÉ ORTIZ, *España: castillos y alcazares.* Madrid, 1956.

FEDDEN, HENRY R., and THOMSON, JOHN, *Crusader Castles.* London, 1957.

FORMILLI, C. J. G., *The Castles of Italy.* London, 1933.

HAHN, HANNO, *Hohenstaufenburgen in Süditalien.* Ingelheim, Germany, 1961.

HARVEY, JOHN, *The Gothic World, 1100–1600.* London, 1950.

HASKINS, CHARLES HOMER, *The Normans in European History.* New York, 1915.

HOLLISTER, C. WARREN, *The Military Organization of Norman England.* Oxford, 1965.

MÜLLER-WARNER, WOLFGANG, *Castles of the Crusades.* New York, 1966.

O'NEIL, B. H. ST. J., *Castles: an Introduction to the Castles of England and Wales.* London, 1973 (Ministry of Works).

ORDERICUS VITALIS, *Ecclesiastical History of England and Normandy,* trans. Thomas Forester, 4 vols. London, 1858.

PEERS, CHARLES, *Pevensey Castle.* London, 1953 (Ministry of Works).

PERKS, J. C., *Chepstow Castle.* London, 1962 (Ministry of Works).

PIPER, OTTO, *Abriss der Burgenkunde.* Leipzig, 1914.

RENN, D. F., *Norman Castles.* London and New York, 1968.

———, *Three Shell Keeps.* London, 1969 (Ministry of Works).

SANDERS, I. J., *English Baronies, a Study of Their Origin and Descent, 1086–1327.* Oxford, 1960.

SCHMIDT, RICHARD, *Burgen des Deutschen Mittelalter.* Munich, 1957.

STENTON, SIR FRANK, *The First Century of English Feudalism.* Oxford, 1961.

THOMPSON, A. HAMILTON, *Military Architecture in England During the Middle Ages.* London, 1912.

TOMKEIEFF, O. G., *Life in Norman England.* New York, 1967.

TOY, SIDNEY, *The Castles of Great Britain.* London, 1953.

Toy, Sidney, *A History of Fortification from 3000 B.C. to A.D. 1700.*
London, 1955.
Tuulse, A., *Castles of the Western World.* London, 1958.
William of Malmesbury, *Historia novella*, trans. K. R. Potter.
London, 1955.

Chapter II. *The Lord of the Castle*

Bloch, Marc, *Feudal Society*, trans. L. A. Manyon, 2 vols.
Chicago, 1964.
————, *Seigneurie française et manoir anglaise.* Paris, 1960.
Boutruche, Robert, *Seigneurie et féodalité*, 2 vols. Paris, 1970.
Cam, Helen, M., *Liberties and Communities in Medieval England.*
Cambridge, England, 1944.
The Cambridge Economic History of Europe, vol. I, *The Agrarian Life of the Middle Ages*, second edition, ed. M. M. Postan. Cambridge, England, 1966.
Cronne, H. A., *The Reign of Stephen, 1135–54, Anarchy in England.*
London, 1970.
* Davis, H. W. C., *England Under the Normans and Angevins.*
* Douglas, David C., *The Norman Achievement.*
* ————, *William the Conqueror.*
Galbert of Bruges, *The Murder of Charles the Good, Count of Flanders*, trans. James Bruce Ross. New York, 1967.
Ganshof, F. L., *Feudalism*, trans. Philip Grierson. New York, 1964.
L'Histoire de Guillaume Maréchal, comte de Striguil et de Pembroke, régent d'Angleterre de 1216 à 1219, ed. Paul Meyer. Paris, 1891–1901.
* Hollister, C. Warren, *The Military Organization of Norman England.*
Keeton, George W., *The Norman Conquest and the Common Law.*
London, 1966.
Morris, William Alfred, *The Medieval English Sheriff to 1300.*
Manchester, England, 1927.

* See earlier citation.

NORGATE, KATE, *The Minority of Henry III*. London, 1912.

PAINTER, SIDNEY, *Feudalism and Liberty*, ed. Fred A. Cazel, Jr. Baltimore, 1961.

————, *Studies in the History of the English Feudal Barony*. Baltimore, 1943.

————, *William Marshal, Knight Errant, Baron and Regent of England*. Baltimore, 1933.

PARIS, MATTHEW, *English History from the Year 1235 to 1273*, trans. J. A. Giles. London, 1854.

* PERKS, J. C., *Chepstow Castle*.

POWICKE, F. M., *King Henry III and the Lord Edward*, 2 vols. Oxford, 1947.

ROUND, J. H., *Feudal England*. London, 1895.

* SANDERS, I. J., *English Baronies*.

STENTON, DORIS M., *English Society in the Early Middle Ages (1066–1307)*. Harmondsworth, England, 1951.

* STENTON, SIR FRANK, *The First Century of English Feudalism*.

STRAYER, JOSEPH R., *Feudalism*. Princeton, 1965.

WILKINSON, B., *Studies in the Constitutional History of the Thirteenth and Fourteenth Centuries*. Manchester, England, 1952.

CHAPTER III. *The Castle as a House*

* BRAUN, HUGH, *The English Castle*.

COLVIN, H. M., ed., *Building Accounts of Henry III*. Oxford, 1971.

LABARGE, MARGARET WADE, *A Baronial Household of the Thirteenth Century*. New York, 1966.

* PARIS, MATTHEW, *English History*.

PARKER, J. H., and TURNER, T. H., *Some Account of Domestic Architecture in England*. Oxford, 1877.

* PERKS, J. C., *Chepstow Castle*.

* TOMKEIEFF, O. G., *Life in Norman England*.

* TOY, SIDNEY, *The Castles of Great Britain*.

Walter of Henley's Husbandry, Together with an Anonymous Husbandry, Seneschaucie, and Robert Grosseteste's Rules, trans. Elizabeth Lamond. London, 1890.

* See earlier citation.

WHITE, LYNN, JR., "Technology Assessment from the Stance of a Medieval Historian." *American Historical Review*, 1974.

WOOD, MARGARET E., *The English Mediaeval House*. London, 1965.

WRIGHT, LAWRENCE, *Clean and Decent*. London, 1960.

CHAPTER IV. *The Lady*

ALBERTUS MAGNUS, *Opera Omnia*, vol. XII, *Quaestiones super de Animalibus*, ed. Bernhardus Geyer. Aschendorff, 1955.

ANDREAS CAPELLANUS, *The Art of Courtly Love*, trans. J. J. Parry. New York, 1941.

Aucassin and Nicolette and Other Medieval Romances and Legends, trans. Eugene Mason. New York, 1958.

BEARD, MARY, *Women as a Force in History*. New York, 1946.

BENTON, JOHN, "Clio and Venus: An Historical View of Medieval Love," in F. X. Newman, ed., *The Meaning of Courtly Love*. Albany, 1968.

———, "The Court of Champagne as a Literary Center." *Speculum*, 1961.

The Book of the Knight of La Tour-Landry, Compiled for the Instruction of His Daughters, ed. Thomas Wright. London, 1868.

The Chronicle of Jocelin of Brakelond, trans. L. C. Jane. New York, 1966.

CREEKMORE, HUBERT, *Lyrics of the Middle Ages*. New York, 1959.

GAUTIER, LÉON, *Chivalry*, trans. D. C. Dunning. London, 1959.

Gesta Stephani, the Deeds of Stephen, trans. K. R. Potter. London, 1955.

HOWARD, G. E., *A History of Matrimonial Institutions*. Chicago, 1904.

* LABARGE, MARGARET WADE, *A Baronial Household*.

LANGLOIS, CHARLES-VICTOR, *La Vie en France au moyen âge de la fin du XIIᵉ au milieu du XIVᵉ siècle d'après des moralistes du temps*. Paris, 1925.

* PAINTER, SIDNEY, *Feudalism and Liberty*.

* See earlier citation.

PAINTER, SIDNEY, *French Chivalry*. Ithaca, N.Y., 1962.

PARIS, GASTON, ed., "Le Lai du Lecheoir," *Romania*, 1879.

* PARIS, MATTHEW, *English History*.

POWER, EILEEN, "The Position of Women," in C. G. Crump and E. F. Jacob, eds., *Legacy of the Middle Ages*. Oxford, 1926.

PRESTAGE, EDGAR, ed., *Chivalry, A Series of Studies to Illustrate Its Historical Significance and Civilizing Influence*. London, 1928.

RENART, JEAN, *L'Escoufle*, ed. Joseph Bédier. Paris, 1913.

————, *Galeran de Bretagne*, ed. Lucien Foulet. Paris, 1925.

Le Roman du castelain de Couci et de la dame de Fayel, ed. John E. Matzke and Maurice Delbouille. Paris, 1936.

SHIRLEY, W. W., ed., *Royal and Other Historical Letters Illustrative of the Reign of Henry III*. Vol. I, 1216–1235. London, 1862.

STENTON, DORIS M., *The English Woman in History*. London, 1959.

VITRY, JACQUES DE, *Exempla, or Illustrative Stories from the Sermones Vulgares*, ed. Thomas F. Crane. London, 1890.

V. *The Household*

BALDWIN, J. F., "The Household Administration of Henry Lacy and Thomas of Lancaster." *English Historical Review*, 1927.

BOYER, MARJORIE N., "Medieval Pivoted Axles." *Technology and Culture*, 1960.

————, "Mediaeval Suspended Carriages." *Speculum*, 1959.

BURTT, JOSEPH T., ed., "Account of the Expenses of John of Brabant and Henry and Thomas of Lancaster, 1292," in *Camden Miscellany*. London, 1853.

"Constitutio Domus Regis" (Establishment of the Royal Household), in *The Course of the Exchequer by Richard, son of Nigel*, trans. and ed. Charles Johnson. London and New York, 1950.

GIUSEPPI, M. S., "The Wardrobe and Household Accounts of Bogo de Clare, 1284–6." *Archaelogica*, 1920.

HENNINGS, MARGARET A., *England Under Henry III, Illustrated from Contemporary Sources*. London, 1924.

* LABARGE, MARGARET WADE, *A Baronial Household*.

* See earlier citation.

MANNYNG, ROBERT, *Handlyng Synne,* and William of Wading-
ton's *Manuel des Pechiez,* ed. Frederick Furnival. London,
1901–3.

OCHINSKY, D., "Medieval Treatises on Estate Management."
Economic History Review, 1956.

* PAINTER, SIDNEY, *William Marshal.*

* PARIS, MATTHEW, *English History.*

RICHARDSON, H. G., "Business Training in Medieval Oxford."
American Historical Review, 1941.

A Roll of the Household Expenses of Richard de Swinfield, ed. John
Webb. London, 1853.

ROUND, J. H., "Castle Watchmen." *English Historical Review,*
1920.

———, "The Staff of a Castle in the Twelfth Century." *English
Historical Review,* 1920.

* STENTON, DORIS M., *English Society in the Early Middle Ages.*

* TOMKEIEFF, O. G., *Life in Norman England.*

TOUT, T. F., *Chapters in the Administrative History of Mediaeval
England,* vols. I and II. Manchester, England, 1920.

TURNER, H. T., ed., *Manners and Household Expenses of England in
the Thirteenth and Fifteenth Centuries.* London, 1841.

* *Walter of Henley's Husbandry.*

CHAPTER VI. *A Day in the Castle*

The Babees' Book, trans. E. Richert. London, 1923.

BATESON, MARY, *Medieval England, 1066–1350.* London, 1905.

* BURTT, JOSEPH T., ed., "Account of the Expenses of John of
Brabant."

COULTON, G. G., *Life in the Middle Ages,* vol. III. Cambridge,
England. 1928–9.

FAIRHOLT, E. W., *Satirical Songs and Poems on Costume.* London,
1899.

* GAUTIER, LÉON, *Chivalry.*

* GIUSEPPI, M. S., "The Wardrobe and Household Accounts of
Bogo de Clare."

* See earlier citation.

The Goodman of Paris, trans. Eileen Power. London, 1928.

HAZLITT, W. CAREW, *Old Cookery Books and Ancient Cuisine.* London, 1902.

* HENNINGS, MARGARET A., *England Under Henry III.*

Historical Works of Giraldus Cambrensis, trans. Thomas Forester and Sir Richard Colt Hoare, ed. Thomas Wright. London, 1913.

* LABARGE, MARGARET WADE, *A Baronial Household.*

* MANNYNG, ROBERT, *Handlyng Synne.*

New Oxford History of Music, vol. II, *Early Medieval Music up to 1300*, ed. Dom Anselm Hughes. London, 1954.

* PARIS, MATTHEW, *English History.*

* RENART, JEAN, *L'Escoufle.*

RENOUARD, YVES, "Le Grand Commerce des vins de Gascogne au moyen âge." *Revue historique*, 1959.

* *Roman du castelain de Couci.*

SALZMAN, L. F., *English Life in the Middle Ages.* London, 1926.

TANNAHILL, REAY, *Food in History.* New York, 1973.

* TOMKEIEFF, O. G., *Life in Norman England.*

* WOOD, MARGARET E., *The English Mediaeval House.*

* *Walter of Henley's Husbandry.*

* WRIGHT, LAWRENCE, *Clean and Decent.*

CHAPTER VII. *Hunting as a Way of Life*

* *Anglo-Saxon Chronicle.*

La Chace dou Serf, ed. Baron Jerome Pichon. Paris, 1840.

Chronicle of Florence of Worcester, trans. Thomas Forester. London, 1854.

* *Chronicle of Jocelin of Brakelond.*

* "Constitutio Domus Regis."

EDWARD, SECOND DUKE OF YORK, *The Master of Game*, ed. W. A. Grohman and F. Baillie. London, 1909.

FOIX, GASTON DE LA, *Le Livre de la chasse*, ed. Paul Lacroix. Paris, 1886.

* See earlier citation.

FREDERICK II, EMPEROR OF GERMANY, *The Art of Falconry*, trans. Casey A. Wood and F. Marjorie Fyfe. Stanford, 1961.

* HENNINGS, MARGARET A., *England Under Henry III.*

HILTON, R. H., *A Medieval Society: the West Midlands at the End of the Thirteenth Century.* London, 1966.

* *Historical Works of Giraldus Cambrensis.*

* LABARGE, MARGARET WADE, *A Baronial Household.*

* ORDERICUS VITALIS, *Ecclesiastical History.*

* PAINTER, SIDNEY, *William Marshal.*

* PARIS, MATTHEW, *English History.*

* PERKS, J. C., *Chepstow Castle.*

PROU, MAURICE, "La Fôret en Angleterre et en France." *Journal des savants*, 1915.

* STENTON, DORIS M., *English Society in the Early Middle Ages.*

* TOMKEIEFF, O. G., *Life in Norman England.*

TRENCH, CHARLES CHENEVIX, *The Poacher and the Squire, a History of Poaching and Game Preservation in England.* London, 1967.

TURNER, G. J., ed., *Select Pleas of the Forest.* London, 1900.

CHAPTER VIII. *The Villagers*

AULT, W. O., *The Self-Directing Activities of Village Communities in Medieval England.* Boston, 1952.

——, "Some Early Village By-Laws." *English Historical Review*, 1930.

BENNETT, H. S., *Life on the English Manor.* Cambridge, England, 1960.

BLOCH, MARC, "Champs et villages." *Annales d'histoire économique et sociale*, 1934.

* ——, *Feudal Society.*

* ——, *Seigneurie française et manoir anglaise.*

——, "Village et seigneurie," *Annales d'histoire économique et sociale.* 1937.

* BOUTRUCHE, ROBERT, *Seigneurie et féodalité.*

* CAM, HELEN M., *Liberties and Communities in Medieval England.*

* See earlier citation.

* *Cambridge Economic History of Europe*, vol. I.

COULTON, G. G., *Medieval Village, Manor and Monastery*. New York, 1960.

DUBY, GEORGES, *Rural Economy and Country Life in the Medieval West*, trans. Cynthia Postan. Columbia, S.C., 1968.

* GANSHOF, F. L., *Feudalism*.

GASQUET, F. A., *Parish Life in Medieval England*. London, 1922.

GRAS, N. S. B., *The Economic and Social History of an English Village, 909–1928*. Cambridge, Mass., 1930.

HARVEY, P. D. A., *A Medieval Oxfordshire Village, Cuxham, 1240 to 1400*. Oxford, 1964.

HILTON, R. H., *Decline of Serfdom in Medieval England*. London, 1969.

* ———, *A Medieval Society*.

HOMANS, G. C., *English Villagers of the Thirteenth Century*. New York, 1960.

———, "The Rural Sociology of Medieval England," in *Past and Present*, 1953.

* KEETON, GEORGE W., *The Norman Conquest and the Common Law*.

LANGLAND, WILLIAM, *Piers the Ploughman*, trans. into modern English by J. F. Goodridge. London, 1959.

LENNARD, R., *Rural England, 1086–1135*. Oxford, 1959.

LEVETT, A. E., *Studies in Manorial History*. Oxford, 1938.

OWST, G. R., *Literature and Pulpit in Medieval England*. Oxford, 1961.

POSTAN, M. M., *Essays on Medieval Agriculture and General Problems of the Medieval Economy*. Cambridge, England, 1973.

———, *The Medieval Economy and Society. An Economic History of Britain, 1100–1300*. Berkeley, 1972.

SEEBOHM, F., *The English Village Community*. London, 1890.

* STENTON, DORIS M., *English Society in the Early Middle Ages*.

STEPHENSON, CARL, "The Problem of the Common Man in Early Medieval Europe." *American Historical Review*, 1946.

* TOMKEIEFF, O. G., *Life in Norman England*.

* *Walter of Henley's Husbandry*.

WHITE, LYNN, JR., *Medieval Technology and Social Change*. Oxford, 1962.

* See earlier citation.

CHAPTER IX. *The Making of a Knight*

BARBER, RICHARD W., *The Knight and Chivalry*. New York, 1970.

* BLOCH, MARC, *Feudal Society*.

CHRÉTIEN DE TROYES, *Perceval le Gallois ou le conte du Graal*, ed. Ch. Potvin. Mons, Belgium, 1866–1871.

* *Chronicle of Jocelin of Brakelond*.

COHEN, GUSTAVE, *Histoire de la chevalerie en France au moyen âge*. Paris, 1949.

DENHOLM-YOUNG, N., "The Tournament in the Thirteenth Century," in *Collected Papers of N. Denholm-Young*. Cardiff, Wales, 1969.

* GANSHOF, F. L., *Feudalism*.

* GAUTIER, LÉON, *Chivalry*.

Girart de Roussillon, chanson de geste, trans. Paul Meyer. Paris, 1884.

* *Histoire de Guillaume Maréchal*.

JOINVILLE, JEAN DE, *Life of St. Louis*, trans. M. R. B. Shaw. Baltimore, 1963.

* LABARGE, MARGARET WADE, *A Baronial Household*.

* MANNYNG, ROBERT, *Handlyng Synne*.

MARCHEGAY, PAUL A., and SALMON, ANDRÉ, eds., *Chroniques des comtes d'Anjou*. Paris, 1856–71.

* PAINTER, SIDNEY, *Feudalism and Liberty*.

* ———, *French Chivalry*.

* ———, *William Marshal*.

* PARIS, MATTHEW, *English History*.

POOLE, AUSTIN L., *Medieval England*, vol. I. Oxford, 1958.

* PRESTAGE, EDGAR, ed., *Chivalry*.

ROGER OF WENDOVER, *Flowers of History*, trans. J. A. Giles, 2 vols. London, 1849.

* *Roman du castelain de Couci*.

* STRAYER, JOSEPH R., *Feudalism*.

* TOMKEIEFF, O. G., *Life in Norman England*.

---

* See earlier citation.

CHAPTER X. *The Castle at War*

Annales Prioratus de Dunstaplia, ed. H. R. Luard. London, 1886.

* BEELER, JOHN, *Warfare in England.*

* ———, *Warfare in Feudal Europe.*

* BROWN, R. ALLEN, *Rochester Castle.*

Chronicon de Mailros, ed. J. Stephenson. Edinburgh, 1845.

FULCHER OF CHARTRES, *A History of the Expedition to Jerusalem, 1095–1127*, trans. Frances Rita Ryan, ed. Harold S. Fink. Knoxville, 1969.

Gesta Francorum et Aliorum Hierosolimitanorum, The Deeds of the Franks and Other Pilgrims to Jerusalem, ed. Rosalind Hill. London, 1962.

* *Gesta Stephani.*

* HENNINGS, MARGARET A., *England Under Henry III.*

A History of Technology, vol. II, ed. Charles Singer, E. J. Holmyard, A. R. Hall, and Trevor Williams. Oxford, 1956.

* HOLLISTER, C. WARREN, *The Military Organization of Norman England.*

LEWIS, ALUN, "Roger Leyburn and the Pacification of England, 1256–7." *English Historical Review*, 1939.

* NORGATE, KATE, *Minority of Henry III.*

NORMAN, A. V. B., *The Medieval Soldier.* New York, 1971.

OMAN, C. W. C., *The Art of War in the Middle Ages.* Ithaca, N.Y., 1953.

* ORDERICUS VITALIS, *Ecclesiastical History.*

* PAINTER, SIDNEY, *William Marshal.*

* PERKS, J. C., *Chepstow Castle.*

* POOLE, AUSTIN L., *Medieval England*, vol. I.

* POWICKE, F. M., *King Henry III and the Lord Edward.*

* TOY, SIDNEY, *A History of Fortification.*

* WHITE, LYNN, JR., "Technology Assessment."

———, "Technology in the Middle Ages," in *Technology and Western Civilization*, ed. Melvin Kranzberg and Carroll W. Purcell, Jr., New York, 1967.

* See earlier citation.

CHAPTER XI. *The Castle Year*

BASKERVILLE, C. R., "Dramatic Aspects of Medieval Folk-Festivals in England." *Studies in Philology*, 1920.

———, "Mummers' Wooing Plays in England." *Modern Philology*, 1924.

* BENNETT, H. S., *Life on the English Manor.*

BRAND, JOHN, *Observations on Popular Antiquities.* London, 1900.

CHAMBERS, E. K., *The English Folk Play.* Oxford, 1933.

———, *The Medieval Stage.* Oxford, 1903.

HAZLITT, W. C., *Faiths and Folklore of the British Isles*, 2 vols. New York, 1965.

* HOMANS, G. C., *English Villagers of the Thirteenth Century.*

LEACH, A. F., *The Schools of Medieval England.* London, 1915.

LECOY DE LA MARCHE, A., *La Chaire française au moyen âge.* Paris, 1886.

* PARIS, MATTHEW, *English History.*

Le Roman de la rose ou Guillaume de Dole, ed. G. Servois. Paris, 1893.

STOW, JOHN, *A Survay of London.* London, 1598 (University Microfilms).

* See earlier citation.

Index